interchange

THIRD EDITION

Jack C. Richards

VIDEO ACTIVITY BOOK

1

PUBLISHED BY THE PRESS SYNDICATE OF THE UNIVERSITY OF CAMBRIDGE
The Pitt Building, Trumpington Street, Cambridge, United Kingdom

CAMBRIDGE UNIVERSITY PRESS
The Edinburgh Building, Cambridge CB2 2RU, UK
40 West 20th Street, New York, NY 10011–4211, USA
477 Williamstown Road, Port Melbourne, VIC 3207, Australia
Ruiz de Alarcón 13, 28014 Madrid, Spain
Nautica Building, The Water Club, Beach Road, Granger Bay, Cape Town 8005, South Africa

http://www.cambridge.org

© Cambridge University Press 2005

First published 1994
Printed in Hong Kong, China
Typeface New Century Schoolbook   *System* QuarkXPress®

ISBN 0 521 60173 8 Student's Book 1
ISBN 0 521 60171 1 Student's Book 1 w/Self-study Audio CD
ISBN 0 521 60172 X Student's Book 1 w/Self-study Audio CD
                            (Korea edition)
ISBN 0 521 60175 4 Student's Book 1A w/Self-study Audio CD
ISBN 0 521 60176 2 Student's Book 1B w/Self-study Audio CD
ISBN 0 521 60177 0 Workbook 1
ISBN 0 521 60178 9 Workbook 1A
ISBN 0 521 60179 7 Workbook 1B
ISBN 0 521 60180 0 Teacher's Edition 1
ISBN 0 521 60185 1 Class Audio Cassettes 1
ISBN 0 521 60182 7 Self-study Audio Cassette 1
ISBN 0 521 60184 3 Class Audio CDs 1
ISBN 0 521 60183 5 Self-study Audio CD 1
ISBN 0 521 60187 8 Lab Guide 1
ISBN 0 521 61340 X Lab Audio CDs 1
ISBN 0 521 95055 4 Class Audio Cassette Sampler
ISBN 0 521 95056 2 Class Audio CD Sampler
ISBN 0 521 95053 8 Classroom Language Posters

Also available
ISBN 0 521 61344 2 Video 1 (DVD)
ISBN 0 521 60188 6 Video 1 (NTSC)
ISBN 0 521 60189 4 Video 1 (PAL)
ISBN 0 521 60191 6 Video Activity Book 1
ISBN 0 521 60192 4 Video Teacher's Guide 1
ISBN 0 521 91481 7 Video Sampler (NTSC)
ISBN 0 521 60238 6 Interchange Third Edition/Passages
                            Placement and Evaluation Package

Forthcoming
ISBN 0 521 60193 2 CD-ROM 1 (PC format)
ISBN 0 521 60181 9 Teacher's Resource Book 1
ISBN 0 521 60239 4 Interchange Third Edition/Passages
                            Placement and Evaluation CD-ROM

Art direction, book design, photo research, and layout services: Adventure House, NYC

INTERCHANGE 1 VIDEO ACTIVITY BOOK THIRD EDITION

● ناشر: انتشارات پیک زبان (نماینده رسمی انتشارات کمبریج در ایران)
● نوبت چاپ: اول ۱۳۸۵
● شمارگان: ۴۰۰۰
● چاپ: کیمیا، تلفن: ۶۶۹۵۵۳۸۵
● لیتوگرافی: نقش آوران رنگین، تلفن: ۸۸۹۶۸۸۳۰
● مرکز پخش: تهران، میدان انقلاب، خیابان اردیبهشت، نرسیده به شهدای ژاندارمری، پلاک ۲۰۴
طبقه سوم، انتشارات پیک زبان، تلفکس: ۶۶۴۸۷۴۳۱ - ۶۶۹۵۳۱۵۵ - ۶۶۹۵۲۵۵۹ - ۶۶۴۱۴۹۰۷
● فروشگاه شماره ۱: تهران، میدان انقلاب، نرسیده به خیابان اردیبهشت، تالار بزرگ کتاب،
شماره ۱۷، کتابفروشی پیک زبان، ۶۶۹۵۳۱۵۵
● فروشگاه شماره ۲: تهران، خیابان کارگر شمالی، مرکز خود اشتغالی شماره یک، موسسه
فرهنگی انتشاراتی زبان افشان، تلفن: ۸۸۹۶۵۲۶۴

E-MAIL: zabanafshan@yahoo.com

Richards, Jack Croft
ریچاردز، جک کرافت، ۱۹۴۳ - م
(اینترچنج ویدئو اکتیویتی بوک ۱ [وان])
Interchange: video activity book 1 [one]/Jack C. Richards. -Third edition
تهران : پیک زبان ، ۱۳۸۴ - ۲۰۰۵م.
۷، ۹۶ ص: مصور (رنگی).

ISBN

فهرستنویسی براساس اطلاعات فیپا
انگلیسی.
افست از روی ویراست سوم ۲۰۰۵: دانشگاه کمبریج.

۱. زبان انگلیسی -- کتابهای درسی برای خارجیان. ۲. ارتباط
بین‌المللی -- مسائل، تمرینها و غیره. ۳. زبان انگلیسی -- خودآموز
دید و شنودی. الف،عنوان: [one] Interchange: video activity book 1.
۴۲۸ /۲۴   PE ۱۱۲۸ /۸۳،۹۷۱:
                              الف ۱۳۸۴
کتابخانه ملی ایران   ۸۴-۲۵۲۲۶م

Plan of Video Activity Book 1

Introduction

■ INTERCHANGE THIRD EDITION

Interchange Third Edition is a revision of
New Interchange, the world's most successful and
popular English course. *Interchange Third Edition*
is a multi-level course in English as a second or
foreign language for young adults and adults. The
course covers the four skills of listening, speaking,
reading, and writing, as well as pronunciation and
vocabulary. Particular emphasis is placed on
listening and speaking. The primary goal of the
course is to teach communicative competence,
that is, the ability to communicate in English
according to the situation, purpose, and roles of
the participants. The language used in
Interchange Third Edition is American English;
however, the course reflects the fact that English
is the major language of international
communication and is not limited to any one
country, region, or culture. Level One is for
students at the beginner or false-beginner level.

Level One builds on the foundations for
accurate and fluent communication already
established in the *Intro* Level by extending
grammatical, lexical, and functional skills. The
syllabus covered in Level One also incorporates
a rapid review of language from the *Intro* Level,
allowing Student's Book 1 to be used with
students who have not studied with *Intro*.

■ THE VIDEO COURSE

Interchange Third Edition Video 1 can be used
with either *Interchange Third Edition* or *New
Interchange.* The Video is designed to
complement the Student's Book or to be used
independently as the basis for a short listening
and speaking course.

As a complement to the Student's Book, the
Video provides a variety of entertaining and
instructive live-action sequences. Each video
sequence provides further practice related to the
topics, language, and vocabulary introduced in
the corresponding unit of the Student's Book.

As the basis for a short, free-standing course,
the Video serves as an exciting vehicle for
introducing and practicing useful conversational
language used in everyday situations.

The Video Activity Book contains a wealth of
activities that reinforce and extend the content of
the Video, whether it is used to supplement the
Student's Book or as the basis for an independent
course. The Video Teacher's Guide provides
thorough support for both situations.

■ COURSE LENGTH

The Video contains sixteen dramatized sequences
and five documentary sequences. These vary
slightly in length, but in general, the sequences
are approximately three minutes each, and
the documentaries are approximately five
minutes each.

The accompanying units in the Video Activity
Book are designed for maximum flexibility and
provide anywhere from 45 to 90 minutes of
classroom activity. Optional activities described
in the Video Teacher's Guide may be used to
extend the lesson as needed.

■ COURSE COMPONENTS

Video

The sixteen video sequences complement Units 1
through 16 of Student's Book 1. Although each
sequence is linked to the topic of the corresponding
Student's Book unit, it presents a new situation
and introduces characters who do not appear in
the text. This element of diversity helps keep
students' interest high and also allows the Video
to be used effectively as a free-standing course.
At the same time, the language used in the video
sequences reflects the structures and vocabulary
of the Student's Book, which is based on an
integrated syllabus that links grammar and
communicative functions.

The five documentaries may be used for review
or at any point in the course. The documentaries
are based on authentic, unscripted interviews
with people in various situations, and serve to
illustrate how language is used by real people in
real situations.

Video Activity Book

The Video Activity Book contains sixteen units based on live-action sequences and five documentary units that correspond to the video sequences and documentaries, and is designed to facilitate the effective use of the Video in the classroom. Each unit includes previewing, viewing, and postviewing activities that provide learners with step-by-step support and guidance in understanding and working with the events and language of the sequence. Learners expand their cultural awareness, develop skills and strategies for communicating effectively, and use language creatively.

Video Teacher's Guide

The Video Teacher's Guide contains detailed suggestions for how to use the Video and the Video Activity Book in the classroom, and includes an overview of video teaching techniques, unit-by-unit notes, and a range of optional extension activities. The Video Teacher's Guide also includes answers to the activities in the Video Activity Book and photocopiable transcripts of the video sequences.

■ VIDEO IN THE CLASSROOM

The use of video in the classroom can be an exciting and effective way to teach and learn. As a medium, video both motivates and entertains students. The *Interchange Third Edition* Video is a unique resource that does the following:

- Depicts dynamic, natural contexts for language use.
- Presents authentic language as well as cultural information about speakers of English through engaging story lines.
- Enables learners to use visual information to enhance comprehension.
- Focuses on the important cultural dimension of learning a language by actually showing how speakers of the language live and behave.
- Allows learners to observe the gestures, facial expressions, and other aspects of body language that accompany speech.

■ WHAT THE VIDEO ACTIVITY BOOK CONTAINS

Each unit of the Video Activity Book is divided into four sections: *Preview*, *Watch the Video*, *Follow-up*, and *Language Close-up*. In general, these four sections include, but are not limited to, the following types of activities:

Preview

Culture The culture previews introduce the topics of the video sequences and provide important background and cultural information. They can be presented in class as reading and discussion activities, or students can read and complete them as homework.

Vocabulary The vocabulary activities introduce and practice the essential vocabulary of the video sequences through a variety of interesting tasks.

Guess the Story/Guess the Facts The Guess the Story (or in some units Guess the Facts) activities allow students to make predictions about characters and their actions by watching the video sequences without the sound or by looking at photos in the Video Activity Book. These schema-building activities help to improve students' comprehension when they watch the sequences with the sound.

Watch the Video

Get the Picture These initial viewing activities help students gain global understanding of the sequences by focusing on gist. Activity types vary from unit to unit, but typically involve watching for key information needed to complete a chart, answer questions, or put events in order.

Watch for Details In these activities, students focus on more detailed meaning by watching and listening for specific information to complete tasks about the story line and the characters.

What's Your Opinion? In these activities, students respond to the sequences by making inferences about the characters' actions, feelings, and motivations, and by stating their opinions about issues and topics.

Follow-up

Role Play, Interview, and Other Expansion Activities This section includes communicative activities based on the sequences in which students extend and personalize what they have learned.

Language Close-up

What Did They Say? These cloze activities focus on the specific language in the sequences by having students watch and listen in order to fill in missing words in conversations.

Grammar and Functional Activities In these activities, which are titled to reflect the structural and functional focus of a particular unit, students practice, in a meaningful way, the grammatical structures and functions presented in the video sequences.

1 First day at class

(هندسی، ونیمرن) ناری تفدم و اداری ایں داد

Preview

1 CULTURE
از تک و بردش

In the United States and Canada, most people have three names:

First name	Middle name	Last name
Anne	Louise	Lucas

In universities, students usually use titles and last names with their teachers:
Hello, Professor Lucas.

How many names do people have in your country?
Do you use titles (Ms., Mrs., Mr., Professor) with last names?
 With first names?
Do you ever call teachers by their first names?

Hello, Professor Anne.

In English, do not use a title with a first name.

2 VOCABULARY Nationalities
مجموع نقات یک زبان، زدوم *ماسب عرب*

Pair work When people first meet, they often talk about nationality.
What do you call people from these countries?

ملتی

Country	Nationality	Country	Nationality	Country	Nationality
Brazil	*Brazilian*	France	French	Mexico	Mexican
Canada	canaddin	Japan	japanis	Spain	spainish
England	Englands	Korea	Koreain	Thailand	thai

3 GUESS THE STORY
معنی حدث - بزدن

Watch the first minute of the video with the sound off.
What do you think happens to the young man?
Check (✓) your answer.

☐ He meets an old friend.
☑ He meets the teacher of his class.
☐ He goes to the wrong classroom.

(استاه کردن)

2

4 GET THE PICTURE

[handwritten Arabic/Persian annotation]

Complete the chart. Then compare with a partner.

First name:
sachiko
Last name:
Tanaka
[handwritten annotation]
Occupation:
student

First name:
Marie
Last name:
Ouellette
[handwritten annotation]
Occupation:
Professor

First name:
Rick
Last name:
?

Occupation:
student

5 WATCH FOR DETAILS

[handwritten annotations]

Check (✓) the correct answers. Then compare with a partner.

[handwritten annotations]

1. Rick is originally from
   - ☑ Mexico.
   - ☐ the United States.
   - ☐ Canada.

2. Rick now lives in
   - ☐ Mexico.
   - ☐ the United States.
   - ☑ Canada.

3. Marie is originally from
   - ☐ France.
   - ☑ Canada.
   - ☐ the United States.

4. Marie teaches
   - ☐ French.
   - ☑ business management.
   - ☐ English.

5. Rick and Sachiko are studying
   - ☐ mathematics.
   - ☐ English.
   - ☑ business management.

6 FORMS OF ADDRESS

How do the people in the video address each other?
Check (✓) the correct answers. Then compare with a
partner. (One item has two answers.)

	First name only	First and last name	Title and last name
1. Marie to Sachiko	☐	☑	☑
2. Marie to Rick	☑	☐	☐
3. Rick to Marie	☐	☐	☑
4. Sachiko to Marie	☐	☑	☑

عقیده ـ نظر ـ رأی ـ گمان

7 WHAT'S YOUR OPINION?

Check (✓) your opinions. Then compare with a partner.

انکار کردن
معرفی کردن

1. Why do you think Rick introduces himself to Marie?
   - ☐ to make a friend
   - ☑ to meet his teacher
   - ☐ other ....

2. When Rick learns that Marie is his teacher, how do you think he feels?
   - ☐ amused
   - ☐ angry
   - ☑ embarrassed
   - ☐ pleased

3. How do you think Marie feels?
   - ☑ amused
   - ☐ angry
   - ☐ embarrassed
   - ☐ pleased

| amused | angry | embarrassed | pleased |

حاکی از رو لبخند خوش آمد از ـ سرفنده اسایل
شرمنده خجالت زده
خرسند خوشحال ـ راضی

تعقیب کردن

Follow-up

روان شناسی نقش کردن ها

8 ROLE PLAY Meeting people

A Group work Imagine you are Rick, Sachiko, or Professor Ouellette.
Write three more questions to ask each other.

1. *Where are you from?*
2. whats your name?
3. How old are you
4. do you have a cadin frends?

گفتن شما چرا کردن

> Where are you from?

B Now introduce yourselves. Have conversations like this:

A: Hello, my name's Rick.
B: Hi, I'm Sachiko.
A: Where are you from, Sachiko?
B: I'm from Japan. . . .

> I'm from Japan.

Language close-up

9 WHAT DID THEY SAY?

Watch the video and complete the conversation. Then practice it.

Rick is introducing himself to Marie Ouellette.

Rick: Hi. _My_ name's Ricardo, but everybody
        calls me _Rick_ .

Marie: Well, nice to _say_ you, Rick.
        say Marie Ouellette.

Rick: It's nice to meet you, Marie. . . . Um,
        Where are you from, Marie?

Marie: I'm from _canada_ .

Rick: Oh, so _you are_ Canadian?

Marie: That's right.

Rick: From what _city_ ?

Marie: Montreal. How _old are_ you?

Rick: I'm originally _Nationality_ Mexico City, but
        my family and I _close_ up here _canada_

Marie: Oh, are you a _friend_ here?

Rick: Yes, I _have_

---

10 QUESTIONS WITH BE

A Complete these questions with **is** or **are**.

1) _Is_ Ms. Tanaka's first name Naomi?
2) _are_ Rick and Sachiko students?
3) _are_ you Canadian, Marie?
4) _Is_ Rick from Argentina?
5) _are_ you a student here, Rick?

B *Pair work* Take turns asking and
answering the questions.

A: Is Ms. Tanaka's first name Naomi?
B: No, it isn't. It's _not_

---

11 WH-QUESTIONS *Getting to know people*

A Complete these questions with **is**, **are**, or **do**.

1) What _is_ Sachiko's last name?
2) Where _are_ Rick and Sachiko from?
3) What _do_ you teach, Professor Ouellette?
4) What _is_ Rick studying?
5) What _are_ you do, Rick?

B *Pair work* Take turns asking and answering
the questions above.

C *Class activity* Now find out about your
classmates. Write four more questions. Then go
around the class and ask them.

1) _What's your name?_
2) _where are you from?_
3) _are you candian?_
4) _have you afriend here?_
5) _are you astdent here Rick?_

2 I need a change!

فیلم و نمایش

Preview

1 CULTURE

از فرهنگ و روزی

THE WORK FORCE IN THE
UNITED STATES AND CANADA

In the United States and Canada, people usually work from
9 A.M. to 5 P.M. Most people get two weeks of vacation a year.
Sometimes people in offices and businesses work late without
extra pay. People also change jobs quite often. The average
person will change careers – not just jobs – two or three times
in a lifetime.

1959	
70%	
30%	
1991	
51%	
49%	

What hours do people work in your country?
How much vacation do they get?
Do they change jobs often?

2 VOCABULARY Occupations

Pair work Who works in the places below? Put the words in the
chart. (One word can go in both columns.) Can you add three
more words?

Hotel	Office
bellhop	computer programmer
secretary	office mangar
cashier	chef
worker	engneir
studnet	teacher

bellhop

computer programmer

secretary

office manager

cashier

chef

6

همس زدن

3 GUESS THE STORY

Watch the first minute of the video with the sound off.
Answer these questions.

1) Where do you think the woman works?

2) What do you think her job is?

3) Do you think she likes her work?

 **Watch the video**

4 GET THE PICTURE

Check (✓) the correct answer. Then compare with a partner.

1) What does Lynn do?
- ☐ She's a hotel worker.
- ☑ She's a manager.
- ☐ She's a salesperson.

فروشنده

2) Why doesn't Lynn like her job?
- ☐ The money isn't good.
- ☐ She doesn't like her boss. رئیس
- ☑ She works long hours.

3) What does Lynn want to do?
- ☐ Work in a hotel.
- ☑ Work for an airline.
- ☐ Work in a restaurant.

5 WATCH FOR DETAILS

Check (✓) **True** or **False**. Then correct the false statements.
Compare with a partner.

	True	False	
1) Lynn works at CompuTech.	☐	☑	Lynn works at AdTech.
2) The company is a computer software company.	☐	☐	
3) Lynn is a manager in customer service.	☐	☐	
4) Lynn works five days a week.	☑	☐	
5) Lynn is studying business.	☐	☐	
6) Bob's friend works in California.	☐	☐	
7) Bob's friend manages a hotel.	☐	☐	

7

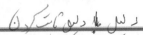

6 GIVING REASONS

Pair work Complete the chart. Look at the pictures and put two possible reasons in each column. (Some reasons can go in both columns.)

Reasons why Lynn doesn't like AdTech	*Reasons why Lynn wants to work in a hotel*
She works on weekends.	*She's interested in hotel management.*

She's interested in
hotel management.

She works on
weekends.

She wants to do
something new.

There's too much
telephone and
computer work.

She likes to travel.

The company is
in a cold climate.

Follow-up

7 ROLE PLAY *Jobs*

A *Pair work* Imagine you work at AdTech.
Talk about your job:

A: Where do you work at AdTech?
B: . . .
A: What do you do in your job?
B: . . .
A: How do you like your job?
B: . . .

B *Group work* Work in groups of four. Choose
a job and ask and answer questions about your
work. Who has the most interesting job?

Language close-up

8 WHAT DID THEY SAY?

Watch the video and complete the conversation. Then practice it.

Paula sees Lynn in the cafeteria at lunch.

Paula: Hi, Lynn! How are ...*you*.... doing?

Lynn: Oh, ... , Paula. Pretty .... , thanks.
How are you?

Paula: Not .... Say, you .... Bob Wallace, don't you?

Lynn: Oh, no, I don't .... so. Hi, ... Lynn Parker.

Bob: Pleased to .... you.

Paula: So, ... everything?

Lynn: .... you really .... to know?

Paula: Of course .... do.

9 WH-QUESTIONS WITH DO; PREPOSITIONS

A Complete the questions in the present tense. Complete the answers with the prepositions **at**, **in**, or **to**. Then practice the conversations.

1) Bob: Where ......*do you work*...... , Lynn?
   Lynn: I work ...*at*... AdTech. It's a computer software company.
   Bob: What .... there?
   Lynn: I'm a manager .... customer service.

2) Bob: Where .... to school, Lynn?
   Lynn: I go .... Franklin University. I'm studying hotel management.

3) Lynn: What .... , Bob?
   Bob: I'm a lawyer.
   Lynn: Oh. Where .... ?
   Bob: I work .... the law firm of Christopher Brown.

Where do you work?

I work at AdTech.

B *Pair work* Now have similar conversations using your own information. (If you don't work, choose a job from page 6.)

10 ASKING ABOUT JOBS

Pair work Bob's friend manages a hotel in Hawaii. Think of three more questions Lynn can ask him about his job. Then ask and answer the questions.

1) *How do you like your job?* ....

2) ....

3) ....

4) ....

Jobs

1 VOCABULARY *Jobs*

Pair work Match the jobs and the pictures.

architect   chef   ✓lawyer   photographer   travel agent
cashier   doctor pianist   teller

1) *lawyer* ....

2) ....

3) ....

4) ....

5) ....

6) ....

7) ....

8) ....

9) ....

2 GUESS THE FACTS

Pair work In this documentary, you are going to meet people with
the jobs above. Which jobs do you think men do? Which do you
think women do?

 **Watch the video**

3 GET THE PICTURE

What do these people do? Write their occupations under the photos.
Then compare with a partner.

1) _reporter_   2) ....   3) ....   4) ....

5) ....   6) ....   7) ....   8) ....

4 WATCH FOR DETAILS

Complete the chart. Then compare with a partner.

Rick Armstrong

1) His job:
....
2) One thing he likes:
....
....
3) One thing that's difficult:
....
....

Sylvia Davis

1) Her job:
....
2) One thing she likes:
....
....
3) One thing that's difficult:
....
....

 **Follow-up**

5 ROLE PLAY   Interview

Class activity Play the role of a reporter and
interview at least three classmates about their
jobs. Have conversations like the one to the right:

A: What do you do?
B: I'm an architect.
A: Do you like your job? . . .

3 At a garage sale

 *Preview*

1 CULTURE

In the United States and Canada, people often sell old things, like furniture, jewelry, or clothing, at a "garage" or "yard" sale. They decide on prices, put the things on tables in their garage or yard, and then put a sign in front of their house. People come to look and maybe to buy. Sometimes the old things are antiques and worth a lot of money.

Do people have garage sales in your country?
What old things do you have at home?
What is one thing that you want to sell?

GARAGE SALE
Saturday, 9 A.M. to 5 P.M. Children's clothes, kitchen items, TV.
257 Maple Avenue

YARD SALE
Sunday, 12 P.M. to 6 P.M. Antiques, books, clock, stereo, bicycle. 89 Shadow Oak Drive

2 VOCABULARY Garage sale items

Pair work Put the words in the chart. Can you add six more words?
Add things from your home.

Kitchen items	Jewelry	Other
		books

books

a bracelet

a watch

a necklace   a motorcycle

dishes

cups and saucers

a camera

3 GUESS THE STORY

A *Watch the video with the sound off.* Which things do you see at the garage sale? Circle them in Exercise 2.

B What do you think the man buys? What does the woman buy? Make a list.

....
....
....
....

....
....
....
....

 Watch the video

4 WHAT'S YOUR OPINION?

In the end, do you think Fred and Susan buy any of these things at the garage sale? Check (✓) **Yes** or **No**. Then compare with a partner.

	Yes	No
1) the camera	☐	☐
2) the motorcycle	☐	☐
3) the necklace	☐	☐
4) the bracelet	☐	☐
5) the watch	☐	☐

5 MAKING INFERENCES

Check (✓) the best answers. Then complete item (4) with your opinion. Compare with a partner.

1) Susan thinks the camera is
   ☐ too old.
   ☐ too expensive.

3) Fred thinks the watch is
   ☐ beautiful.
   ☐ too expensive.

2) Fred thinks the necklace is
   ☐ beautiful.
   ☐ just all right.

4) The man tells his wife that ....
....
....

Follow-up

6 GARAGE SALE

A *Pair work* Imagine you are at a garage sale. Number the sentences below (1 to 6) to make conversations. Then practice the conversations.

1) .... And how much are these earrings?
   ...1... Hello. Can I help you?
   .... It's twelve dollars.
   .... Yes, how much is this bracelet?
   .... They're twenty dollars.
   .... Thanks. I'll think about it.

2) .... Can I help you?
   .... Oh, that's pretty expensive.
   .... OK. I'll take it.
   .... Yes, how much is this watch?
   .... Well, how about thirty dollars?
   .... It's forty dollars.

B *Class activity* Plan a class garage sale. Form two groups. Make a list of things your group will sell, and give each item a price.

Items for sale	Price
....	....
....	....
....	....
....	....
....	....

Now have the garage sale:

Group A: You are the sellers. Try to sell everything on your list to Group B. Then change roles and decide what to buy from Group B.

Group B: You are the buyers. Ask questions and decide what to buy. Then change roles and try to sell everything on your list to Group A.

Language close-up

7 WHAT DID THEY SAY?

Watch the video and complete the conversation. Then practice it.

Fred and Susan are looking at things at the garage sale.

Fred: Hey, Susan, how do you ......*like*...... this?

Susan: Oh, ..., Fred.

Fred: Oh, come on. It's only a ....!

Susan: .... you really .... it, Fred?

Fred: No, I guess .... right.

Vendor: Can I .... you?

Fred: No, thanks .... We're just ....

Susan: Oh, Fred, ... over here. Just look at this lovely, old .... !

Fred: Yeah, it's ....

Susan: It's .... just OK, Fred. It's very .... !

8 EXPRESSING OPINIONS

Fred says these sentences. What do they mean in the video?
Check (✓) the correct answer. Then compare with a partner.

1) How do you like this?
   - ☐ Can you believe this?
   - ☐ What do you think of this?

2) Oh, come on.
   - ☐ Please let me [buy it].
   - ☐ Are you kidding?

3) Yeah, it's OK.
   - ☐ I like it a little.
   - ☐ The price is reasonable.

4) Oh, that's not bad.
   - ☐ It's nice.
   - ☐ The price is reasonable.

5) Susan, are you kidding?
   - ☐ I don't believe it!
   - ☐ Let's go!

9 HOW MUCH *AND* HOW OLD

A Complete the conversations with **how much is (are)** or **how old is (are)**.

1) A: *How much is* .... this necklace?
   B: It's only $10.
   A: .... it?
   B: It's twenty years old.

2) A: .... these books?
   B: They're $2 each.
   A: And .... they?
   B: They're about ten years old.

3) A: .... these shoes?
   B: About two years old, I think.
   A: .... they?
   B: They're $20.

B **Pair work** Practice the conversations. Use items of your own.

15

4 What kind of movies do you like?

1 CULTURE

Today, there is a video store in almost every neighborhood in the United States and Canada. Nowadays, many people don't go to the movies very often. Instead they prefer to rent a video and watch it at home. Video stores are large, with every type of video for rent. You can also rent videos in some supermarkets.

Number of stores renting videos
(U.S. and Canada)
1993   82,500
1983   13,000

Do people go to the movies a lot in your country?
Do they rent videos?
What is your favorite movie or video?

Average Price of
A MOVIE TICKET   A VIDEO RENTAL
$5.00 $2.50

2 VOCABULARY Kinds of movies

What kind of movies or videos do you like? Check (✓) your opinions. Then compare answers in groups.

Indiana Jones and the Last Crusade

WHAT'S YOUR OPINION?				
	I like them.	They're OK.	I don't like them very much.	I can't stand them.
adventure movies	☐	☐	☐	☐
classic films	☐	☐	☐	☐
comedies	☐	☐	☐	☐
horror films	☐	☐	☐	☐
science-fiction movies	☐	☐	☐	☐
suspense movies	☐	☐	☐	☐

Dracula

Eyes of Laura Mars

Star Trek III

Heaven Help Us

3 GUESS THE STORY

Watch the first two minutes of the video with the sound off.
Answer these questions.

1) Are the young men friends? 2) What are they doing? 3) What's the problem?

Watch the video

4 GET THE PICTURE

Check (✓) **True** or **False**. Then compare with a partner.

	True	False
1) Pat, Alfredo, and Bill all like movies.	☐	☐
2) Nobody likes science fiction.	☐	☐
3) They can't agree on a movie.	☐	☐
4) They decide to go to a country and western concert.	☐	☐

Pat   Alfredo   Bill

5 MAKING INFERENCES

What do Pat, Bill, and Alfredo like? Write **Y** (yes), or **N** (no). Then compare in groups. (Sometimes they don't say exactly, but try to give your opinion.)

	Pat	Bill	Alfredo
Movies			
science fiction	Y	N	
suspense thrillers		Y	
classic films			....
horror films			....
westerns		....	
Music		....	
country and western		....	
jazz		....	

6 WHAT'S THE PROBLEM?

Pair work Answer these questions.

1) Which person is difficult to please?
2) Do you know anyone like this?

Alfredo   Bill   Pat

 Follow-up

7 FINISH THE STORY

Group work What do you think happens in the end?
Finish the story.

8 MAKING PLANS

Group work Plan what to do this evening. Choose
one of these activities. Give your opinions like this:

There's a great .... tonight at ....
Do you really like .... ?
That sounds good. How about you, ... ?
I don't really like ....
Well, what kind of .... do you like?

9 WHAT DID THEY SAY?

Watch the video and complete the conversation. Then practice it.

Bill, Alfredo, and Pat are trying to decide how to spend the evening.

Bill: So, . . . what ..do.. we ..do.. now?

Alfredo: What .... is it?

Bill: .... o'clock.

Pat: Look, ... all like .... Why don't we
.... a video and .... it at my .... ?

Bill: That's .... a bad .... , Pat.

Alfredo: It's .... with ....

Pat: Well, then, ... on! . . . Now here .... some
great ....-fiction movies! .... do
you .... , Bill?

Bill: Uh, I can't .... sci-fi. How .... a good
.... thriller?

Pat: Uh . . . Alfredo, ... about you? .... do you
.... of science .... ?

Alfredo: Oh, it's ....

Alfredo   Bill   Pat

10 OBJECT PRONOUNS

A Fill in the blanks with **him**, **her**, **it**, or **them**.

1) A: Do you like horror films?
   B: No, I can't stand ...*them*.... .

2) A: Who's your favorite actress?
   B: Michelle Pfeiffer. I like .... a lot.

3) A: Do you like rap music?
   B: Yes, I like .... a lot.

4) A: What do you think of Robert DeNiro?
   B: I don't like .... at all.

5) A: Do you like westerns?
   B: No, I don't like .... very much.

6) A: What do you think of science fiction?
   B: I like .... a lot.

B *Pair work* Take turns asking and answering the questions above.
Give your own opinions.

11 EXPRESSING LIKES AND DISLIKES

Pair work Take turns giving opinions about movies, actors, and actresses.
Your partner responds with surprise, as in the conversations below.

1) A: I can't stand science fiction!
   B: Really?

2) A: I love Julia Roberts.
   B: Are you kidding?

3) A: I hate old movies.
   B: Is that right?

4) A: I think Tom Cruise is fantastic.
   B: Do you really like Tom Cruise?

What's your favorite kind of music?

Preview

1 VOCABULARY Kinds of music

Class activity In this documentary, some
people are going to talk about music. How
many kinds of music can you think of?
List them.

 **Watch the video**

2 GET THE PICTURE

How many different kinds of music do people talk about? Check (✓) them.
Then compare with a partner.

☐ classical   ☐ jazz   ☐ rap
☑ country and western ☐ new wave   ☐ rhythm and blues (R & B)
☐ folk   ☐ pop   ☐ rock

3 WATCH FOR DETAILS

A What kind(s) of music do these people like? Check (✓) all correct
answers. Then compare with a partner.

	1	2	3	4	5	6
country and western	☑	☐	☐	☐	☐	☐
jazz	☐	☐	☐	☐	☐	☐
rock	☐	☐	☐	☐	☐	☐
classical	☐	☐	☐	☐	☐	☐
new wave	☐	☐	☐	☐	☐	☐

B Which people play a musical instrument? Write **S** for saxophone,
G for guitar, or **P** for piano. Then compare with a partner. (One person
doesn't play an instrument.)

saxophone

guitar

piano

1) .... 2) .... 3) .... 4) .... 5) ....

4 THE REPORTER'S QUESTIONS

What interview questions does the reporter ask? Check (✓) them.
Then compare with a partner.

✓ How often do you get to go to nightclubs?
☐ What's your favorite kind of music?
☐ Do you like rap?
☐ How often do you listen to live music?
☐ What's your least favorite kind of music?
☐ Do you like classical music?

☐ Do you play a musical instrument (yourself)?
☐ What do you think of country and western music?
☐ Where's a good place to go dancing?
☐ How often do you go dancing?
☐ What's your favorite nightclub?

Follow-up

5 CLASS INTERVIEW

A *Class activity* Use the questions in Exercise 4
to interview at least three classmates. Have
conversations like this:

A: How often do you go to nightclubs?
B: About twice a week.
A: What's your favorite kind of music?
B: Country.

B Now tell about the people you interviewed. What kinds of
music are the most popular? Least popular?

family picnic

 **Preview**

1 CULTURE

In the United States and Canada, 97 percent of all people say that family is the most important part of life. But people in the U.S. and Canada move often, and children often leave home at age 18. Many families only see each other on important holidays or at family parties.

- Six percent of all families move every year.
- On an average day, 116,438 people move.
- People often live far away from their parents and grandparents.
- Only 36 percent of families see their relatives once a week.

In the U.S. and Canada, 70 percent of all husbands and wives say they're happy with each other.

In your country, when do children leave home?
Do children live near their parents and grandparents?
When do families see each other?

2 VOCABULARY *Family*

Pair work How are these people related to Jane? Fill in the blanks in her family tree.

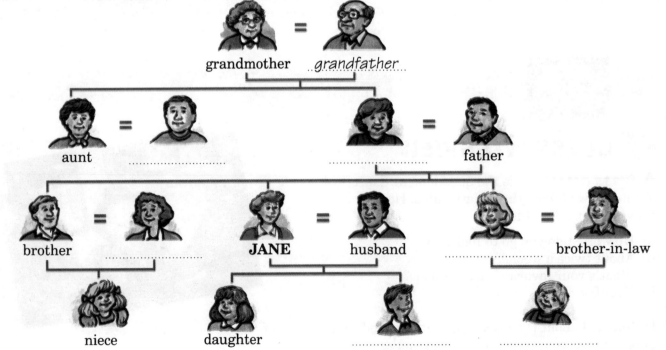

3 GUESS THE STORY

Watch the first minute of the video with the sound off.
The young man takes his friend Betsy to a family picnic.
Who do you think she meets? Look at the photo and list
five more people.

1) *his mother*   4) ....

2) ....   5) ....

3) ....   6) ....

 **Watch the video**

4 GET THE PICTURE

Who's at the picnic? Check (✓) **Yes** or **No**. Then compare with
a partner.

	Yes	No
1) Rick's parents	✓	☐
2) his brother	☐	☐
3) his brother's wife	☐	☐
4) his niece	☐	☐
5) his grandparents	☐	☐
6) his younger sister	☐	☐
7) his older sister	☐	☐
8) his aunt	☐	☐

5 WATCH FOR DETAILS

Check (✓) the correct answer. Then compare with a partner.

1) Rick's grandmother lives in
   ☑ Mexico.
   ☐ New Mexico.

2) Rick has
   ☐ one brother and a sister.
   ☐ one brother and two sisters.

3) Rick's brother Freddy
   ☐ is a doctor.
   ☐ owns a business.

4) Freddy's wife Linda manages
   ☐ a boutique.
   ☐ a bookstore.

5) Angela is
   ☐ three years old.
   ☐ four years old.

6) Rick knows Betsy from
   ☐ work.
   ☐ night school.

6 WHAT'S YOUR OPINION?

Pair work Read the culture box on page 22 again. Is Rick's family like most families in the United States and Canada? How is it the same and how is it different?

Follow-up

7 YOUR FAMILY

A *Pair work* Is your family like Rick's? Tell about your family and find out about your partner's. Ask questions like these:

Are you living with your parents right now?
Are you married?
Do you have any children?
How old are they?
Do you have any brothers and sisters?
Are they still going to school or are they working?

B Draw a simple picture (or show your partner a photo) of your family. Your partner will ask questions about each person.

Is this your sister?
What does she do?
Is she studying English?

8 AN INTERESTING PERSON

A *Pair work* Find out about your partner's most interesting relative or friend. Ask questions like these:

Who's your most interesting relative or friend?
What's his/her name?
What does he/she do?
Where is he/she living at the moment?
How old is he/she?
Is he/she married?

B Now tell another classmate about the person like this:

Yong Su has an interesting cousin.
Her name is Son Hee.
She owns a travel agency.
She's from Seoul.
She's working in New York at the moment.
She's 30 years old.

Language close-up

9 WHAT DID THEY SAY?

Watch the video and complete the conversation. Then practice it.

Betsy and Rick are arriving at the picnic.

Betsy: So, how many ....*people*.... are there in your
......*family*......, Rick?

Rick: A ...., if you count all my ....

Betsy: Do they all .... here in the .... now?

Rick: Oh, ... I have relatives in .... My
grandmother and .... are
there, and my older ...., too.

Betsy: How many .... do you have?

Rick: ...., plus an older .... There's my
.... Freddy over there with his
.... Linda.

Betsy: Oh, really. What do they .... ?

Rick: Freddy .... an import-export business, and
Linda manages .... boutique.

Betsy: Is that their .... ?

Rick: Yeah. Her ....'s Angela.

---

10 PRESENT CONTINUOUS VS. SIMPLE PRESENT
Asking about relatives

A Complete the conversation using the present continuous or simple present.
Then practice with a partner.

A: Do all of your relatives live in the United States?

B: No, I ....*have*........... (have) relatives in Mexico. My grandparents and
older sister .... (live) there.

A: What does your sister do? Does she have a job?

B: No, she .... (work) right now. She .... (go) to school.

A: Really? What is she studying?

B: She .... (study) English literature. She .... (love) it.

A: What about your grandparents? Are they still working or are they retired?

B: They .... (work)! And they're both 80 years old!

B *Class activity* Now write similar questions of your own. Then go
around the class and interview your classmates about their families.

1) *Do your parents live in . . . ?* ....

2) ....

3) ....

4) ....

25

I like to stay in shape.

1 CULTURE

In the United States and Canada, most people nowadays think regular exercise is important. They exercise at home, or at a gym or health club. They play sports after school, after work, and on weekends. They also bicycle, walk, swim, or jog. People exercise for different reasons: to lose weight, to stay in shape, or just to relax.

Do you exercise or play sports?
What sports are popular in your country?

In the U.S. and Canada:

Thirty-five percent of people exercise every day.

Eighteen percent of people play team sports regularly.

2 VOCABULARY *Sports and exercise*

A Pair work Here are some things people do to stay in shape. Write the words under the pictures.

aerobics   basketball   ✓jogging   soccer   swimming   volleyball

1) jogging............................

2) ....

3) ....

4) ....

5) ....

6) ....

B Put the words in the chart. Can you add two more words?

Individual activities		Team sports	
jogging............		....	
....		....	

26

3 GUESS THE STORY

Watch the first minute of the video with the sound off.
Who do you think likes to exercise more, the woman or the man?

I like to stay in shape.

 Watch the video

4 GET THE PICTURE

Check (✓) **True** or **False**. Correct the false statements. Then compare
with a partner.

	True	False	
1) Mark is a friend of Anne's.	☐	☐	....
2) Mark really likes to exercise.	☐	☐	....
3) Anne is in better shape than Mark.	☐	☐	....

5 WATCH FOR DETAILS

A How does Mark stay in shape? Check (✓)
the things he *says* he does.

B Which things do you think he *really* does?
Circle them. Then compare with a partner.

☐ He jogs to stay in shape.

☐ He gets up early.

☐ He bicycles.

☐ He does aerobics.

☐ He swims.

☐ He goes to the health club.

☐ He takes long walks.

☐ He plays tennis.

☐ He plays team sports.

6 WHAT'S YOUR OPINION?

Pair work What kind of person is Anne? What kind of person is Mark? Choose at least one word for each person.

Anne	Mark
....	....
....	....
....	....

friendly   intelligent

polite   pushy

Follow-up

7 INTERVIEW

A Pair work Add three questions to the list about sports and exercise.

1) What kinds of sports do you play?
2) What kinds of exercise do you do?
3) Are you in good shape?

4) ....
5) ....
6) ....

B Take turns asking and answering your questions. Your partner will answer playing the role of Anne or Mark.

8 HOW ABOUT YOU?

A Complete the chart. Then compare with a partner.

Things you sometimes do	Things you don't usually do
I sometimes ..... after school.	I don't usually ..... on the weekend.
....	....
....	....
Things you never do	
I never go ..... in the morning.	
....	
....	

B Class activity Who in the class likes to exercise? Who doesn't? Make a class chart.

Language close-up

9 WHAT DID THEY SAY?

Watch the video and complete the conversation.
Then practice it.

Anne is jogging in the park when Mark introduces himself.

Mark: Hi there. Nice ....*day*...., isn't it?

Anne: Oh, yes, very ....

Mark: Do you .... come out here this .... ?

Anne: Usually. I like to stay in ....

Mark: I do, too. I .... get up around ....
o'clock.

Anne: Oh, ... ?

Mark: Yeah. I .... start with some
.... There's a ....
aerobics program on TV at ....

Anne: No .... ! I guess you really do ....
to stay in shape.

Mark: Hey, ... days a .... I go straight to my
health club after ....

---

10 ADVERBS OF FREQUENCY

A Put the adverbs in the correct place. Write the sentences.

1) I get up before 5 A.M. (never)
   I never get up before 5 A.M.

2) I don't have a big breakfast. (usually)
   ....

3) I play tennis after work. (sometimes)
   ....

4) I take a long walk on the weekend. (often)
   ....

5) I watch TV. (never)
   ....

6) I jog in the morning. (always)
   ....

B Imagine you are Mark. Change the frequency adverbs in the
sentences where necessary. Compare with a partner.

C How often do you do these things? Use the phrases below or ones of
your own. Then compare with a partner.

every evening	very often	about three times a month
twice a week	once a year	every day

1) go to sleep by 10 P.M.
   ....

2) work late
   ....

3) ride a bicycle
   ....

4) do aerobics
   ....

How was your trip to San Francisco?

 **Preview**

1 CULTURE

More than two million people visit San Francisco every year. San Francisco is famous for its shops, its restaurants, its beautiful old buildings, and its cable cars. San Francisco's Chinatown is an important part of the city. There are more than 80,000 people living in Chinatown. San Francisco is also famous for fog and hills. In fact, the city is built on 43 hills!

Do you know anything else about San Francisco?
Would you like to visit San Francisco?
What cities in North America would you like to visit?

There are more than 3,300 restaurants in San Francisco!

2 VOCABULARY *Places in San Francisco*

Pair work How much do you know about San Francisco?
Write the names under the pictures.

Fisherman's Wharf   Chinatown   The Japanese Tea Garden
The Golden Gate Bridge   ✓A cable car   Ghirardelli Square

1) *A cable car*

2) ....

3) ....

4) ....

5) ....

6) ....

30

3 GUESS THE STORY

Watch the video with the sound off. Which of the things in Exercise 2 do you think the woman and her husband see? Write a check (✓) next to them.

Watch the video

4 GET THE PICTURE

A Look at your answers to Exercise 3. Did you guess correctly?

B Correct the mistakes in Phyllis's travel diary. Then compare with a partner.

DAY	NOTES
FRIDAY ~~sight-seeing~~ work	Fisherman's Wharf was my favorite place!
SATURDAY work	
SUNDAY morning: sight-seeing	

5 WATCH FOR DETAILS

What did Phyllis and her husband do in these places? Check (✓) the correct answers. Then compare with a partner.

1) Ghirardelli Square
   - ☐ They bought some clothes.
   - ☐ They bought some postcards.

2) Fisherman's Wharf
   - ☐ They bought some souvenirs.
   - ☐ They had lunch.

3) Golden Gate Park
   - ☐ They visited a tea garden.
   - ☐ They had lunch.

4) Chinatown
   - ☐ They walked for hours.
   - ☐ They visited a temple.

Follow-up

6 A DAY IN SAN FRANCISCO

A *Group work* Which things to see in San Francisco seem most interesting to you? Number them from 1 to 6 (1 = the most interesting).

Ghirardelli Square

Fisherman's Wharf

A cable car

Chinatown

Golden Gate Park

The Japanese Tea Garden

B Plan an afternoon in San Francisco. Choose three places to visit or things to do.

7 WHAT'S YOUR OPINION?

A *Pair work* What do you like to do when you visit a new city? Number them from 1 to 5. Can you add three things to the list?

.... go sight-seeing

.... eat at local restaurants

.... buy souvenirs

.... take photographs

.... go shopping

1) ....

2) ....

3) ....

B Now compare answers with another pair. Have conversations like this:

A: Do you like to go shopping?
B: No, I don't. I hate to go shopping.

Language close-up

8 WHAT DID THEY SAY?

Watch the video and complete the conversation. Then practice it.

Phyllis and Yoko are on their way to work.

Yoko: Hi, Phyllis.
Phyllis: Hi, Yoko. ...How... have you been?
Yoko: Oh, ... How .... you?
Phyllis: Great! Just .... !
Yoko: So, ... was your .... to San Francisco?
Phyllis: Fantastic! We really .... it.
Yoko: Well, that .... surprise me. I love to ....
          San Francisco. Uh, so, your .... went with you?
Phyllis: Yes. I .... on Friday, and Bill had business to do in
          the .... , too.
Yoko: Oh, that's .... So, what did you do over the .... ?
Phyllis: We went .... together all day Saturday and
          Sunday ....
Yoko: Oh, really? .... me about it.

9 PAST TENSE Describing a trip

A Fill in the blanks with the correct past tense forms of the verbs in
parentheses. Then practice the conversations.

1) Yoko: Tell me about your trip to San Francisco.
   Phyllis: Well, we ...*did*... (do) a lot of interesting things. Naturally,
             we .... (start) Saturday morning with a ride on a cable car.
   Yoko: Naturally! And then?
   Phyllis: Then we .... (go) straight to Ghirardelli Square to do some shopping.
   Yoko: Isn't it wonderful? I .... (go) there the last time I .... (be)
             in San Francisco.

2) Yoko: .... you .... (visit) Alcatraz Island?
   Phyllis: No, we .... (have / not) time.
   Yoko: Oh, what .... you .... (do) then?
   Phyllis: We .... (take) a cab to Golden Gate Park.
   Yoko: Great! .... you .... (see) the Japanese Tea Garden?
   Phyllis: Oh, yes, it .... (be) really beautiful. But, to tell the truth,
             the thing we .... (like) best .... (be) Chinatown.

B *Pair work* Have similar conversations about a real or imaginary trip of
your own. Start like this:

A: I went to . . .
B: Really! Tell me about your trip. . . .

33

8 Are you sure it's all right?

 *Preview*

1 CULTURE

In the United States and Canada, people often invite friends to their homes for a meal or a party. Here are some simple rules to follow:
- When someone invites you to dinner, do not bring anyone with you. Your host will tell you if you can bring a guest, such as your husband or wife.
- When someone invites you to a party, you can often bring a friend. But always call your host first to ask if it's OK.

PARTY

Date: June 15
Time: 8:00 P.M.
Place: 26 Elm St.
Apt. 2C
Bring a Friend!

In your country, do people often invite friends to their home for dinner?
Is it OK to bring a friend to dinner? To a party?

2 VOCABULARY Places

Pair work Write the numbers of the places on the map. (There is one extra place.)

1) There's a **coffee shop** on the corner of Hennepin and Lagoon.
2) There's a **movie theater** on Hennepin, just before the coffee shop.
3) There's a **drugstore** across the street from the movie theater.
4) There's a **parking lot** on Lagoon, next door to the coffee shop.
5) Your friend's **apartment building** is across the street from the parking lot.

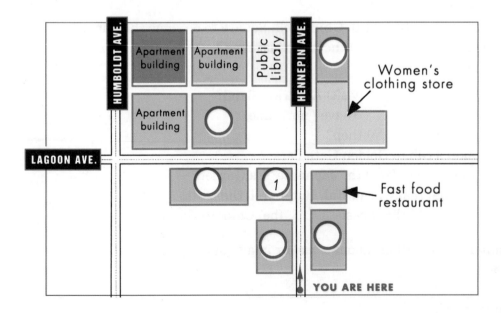

34

3 GUESS THE STORY

Watch the first minute of the video with the sound off.
These people are going to a party. What do you think
happens? Check (✓) your answer.

☐ They get lost.
☐ They go on the wrong day.
☐ They arrive too late.

 Watch the video

4 GET THE PICTURE

A Check (✓) the correct answers. Then compare with a partner.

	Katy	Bill	Pat	Sandy
1) Who is having a party?	☐	☐	☐	☐
2) Who did (s)he invite?	☐	☐	☐	☐
3) Who didn't (s)he invite?	☐	☐	☐	☐
4) Who is a good friend of Katy's?	☐	☐	☐	☐

B What mistake do Bill, Pat, and Sandy make? Did you guess
correctly in Exercise 3?

5 WATCH FOR DETAILS

Correct the mistakes below. Then compare with a partner.

         Sandy   *Katy's*
Pat, Bill, and ~~Katy~~ are going to a party at ~~Sandy's~~ apartment. The

party is very formal. Pat doesn't remember the exact address, but he

remembers there's a coffee shop just before you turn. When they arrive,

they don't hear any music. It's a little late. The party was last week.

6 WHAT'S YOUR OPINION?

Pair work Answer these questions.

1) Is it OK for Bill to take
   Sandy and Pat to the party?
   ☐ Yes, it's fine.
   ☐ No. It's not a good idea.
   ☐ I'm not sure.

2) How do you think Katy feels
   when her friends arrive?
   ☐ amused
   ☐ angry
   ☐ surprised
   ☐ other ....

3) How do you think Pat and
   Sandy feel?
   ☐ embarrassed
   ☐ angry
   ☐ amused
   ☐ other ....

 *Follow-up*

7 INVITING

Group work Invite two or three classmates to one of these activities.

| the beach | the movies | a party | a soccer game |

Start like this:

A: *(Name of classmate)* invited me to .... on
   Sunday. Do you want to come?
B: Are you sure it's OK?
A: Of course it is! .... is a good friend of mine.
C: Well, I don't know. Why don't you ask .... first? . . .

8 ROLE PLAY *A surprise guest*

A ***Group work*** Work in groups of four. Play the roles
of Katy, Sandy, Bill, and Pat. Knock on Katy's door and
act out the situation three times.

1) The first time, act out the conversation just like
   in the video.
2) The second time, imagine Katy is busy and
   doesn't want company.
3) The third time, make up your own ending.

B Now act out your third conversation for the
class. Who has the best ending?

Language close-up

9 WHAT DID THEY SAY?

Watch the video and complete the conversation. Then practice it.

Pat, Bill, and Sandy are going to Katy's party. Pat is asking for directions.

Pat: OK. Well, we're at the ......*corner*...... of 31st Street. ...*Now*... what?

Bill: Well, I don't remember her .... ,
        but I know she lives .... here.

Pat: Fine. But do I go .... , right, or straight
        .... ?

Bill: .... ahead. . . . I remember there's
        a .... theater just before you ....

Pat: Hey, is .... it?

Bill: No, I .... think so. . . . There was a coffee
        shop .... door and a drugstore ....
        the street.

Sandy: Oh, I don't see a .... Well, there's a Vietnamese
        .... with a bookstore .... to it.

Pat: Yeah, and no .... shop either. Hey, look! There's another
        movie theater up ahead on the ....

Bill: Great! .... a drugstore.

10 LOCATIONS

A Look at the map of Katy's neighborhood. Answer
the questions using these prepositions.

across from   near   next to
on the corner of   on

1) Where's the Suburban World Theater?
   It's across from the Vietnamese restaurant.

2) Where's Border's Book Shop?
   ....

3) Where's Figlio's Restaurant?
   ....

4) Where's the Rainbow Cafe?
   ....

5) Where's the clothing store?
   ....

B *Pair work* Now ask similar questions about
places near your school.

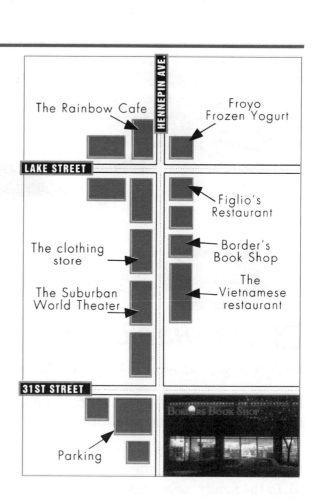

Documentary 3
In a suburban home

1 VOCABULARY Guess the rooms of a house

Pair work Match the words and the photos.

child's bedroom   family room   ✓kitchen
dining room   guest room   living room

1) *kitchen* ....

2) ....

3) ....

4) ....

5) ....

6) ....

Watch the video

2 GET THE PICTURE

A Look at your answers to Exercise 1. Were they correct?

B What is one thing the Bartlett family does in each room? Complete the sentences. Then compare with a partner.

1) In the kitchen, they ....
2) In the dining room, they ....
3) In the family room, they ....

3 WATCH FOR DETAILS

Write down all of the things you see in each room. Then combine answers in groups. Which group has the most things on its list?

1) the kitchen	2) the dining room	3) the living room	4) Matthew's room
a sink			
5) the guest room	6) Daniel's room	7) the large bedroom	8) the family room

4 WHAT'S YOUR OPINION?

Pair work Answer these questions.

1) Do you like the Bartletts' home? Name one thing that you like. Is there anything you don't like?
2) Is the Bartlett home like homes in your country? How is it different?

Follow-up

5 YOUR HOME

Group work Find out about the homes or apartments your classmates live in. Ask questions like these:

1) Do you live in a city?
2) How big is your home?
3) What are some interesting things in your home?
4) What's your favorite room?

Do you live in a city?

No, I live on a farm.

9 Help is coming.

1 CULTURE

To protect their homes against crime, people in the United States and Canada:
- Put special locks on their doors.
- Leave lights on when they go out.
- Have a "peephole" (or hole in the door) to see who's outside.
- Buy an alarm that makes noise if someone opens the door or window.
- Buy a dog.

What other ways can you protect your home?
How do people protect their homes in your country?

On an average day in the U.S., people spend over $2 million on home security.

2 VOCABULARY *Physical appearance*

A *Pair work* Write the words and phrases in the chart. (One of the words can go in two places.) Can you add two more words or phrases?

✓early forties   late forties   short   blond   elderly
long   curly   tall   bald

Age	Height	Hair
early forties		

B List two ways to describe the man and two to describe the woman.

The man	The woman
late forties	

40

3 GUESS THE STORY

Watch the first minute of the video with the sound off.
Who do you think comes to the couple's house?

 Watch the video

4 GET THE PICTURE

What really happens? Check (✓) your answer. Then compare
with a partner.

- ☐ Strange men come to the door.
- ☐ Dave's cousin comes to visit.
- ☐ The prisoners come to the house.
- ☐ Some friends come to visit.

5 WATCH FOR DETAILS

Put the pictures in order (1 to 6). Then write the correct sentence
under each picture. Compare with a partner.

✓Sarah and Dave are reading.   Sarah is looking at the minivan.
 Dave is calling the police.   The men are getting out of the minivan.
 The men are standing in the driveway. The men are introducing themselves to Sarah and Dave.

....

....

....

....

....

....

Sarah and Dave are
reading.

....

....

....

....

6 DESCRIBING SOMEONE

A Circle the correct answers. Then compare with a partner.

	George		Don	
1) Age	twenties	(forties)	twenties	forties
2) Hair color	blond	brown	blond	brown
3) Height	tall	short	tall	short
4) Type of shirt	short-sleeved	long-sleeved	short-sleeved	long-sleeved
5) Other	baseball cap	no hat	baseball cap	no hat
	glasses	no glasses	glasses	no glasses

B What else can you add about George and Don? Compare your descriptions. Who has the best description?

 *Follow-up*

7 THE RIGHT DECISION?

Pair work Sarah and Dave call the police. What is the best thing to do in a situation like this?

☐ Call the police.
☐ Open the door and ask, "Who's there?"
☐ Call a friend or relative.
☐ other ....

8 WHAT HAPPENS NEXT?

A **Group work** What do you think happens when the police arrive? Write out the conversation between Sarah, Dave, and the police. Start like this:

Officer: Is there a problem here?
Dave: Well, uh, . . .

B **Class activity** Act out your conversation for the class.

42

Language close-up

9 WHAT DID THEY SAY?

Watch the video and complete the conversation. Then practice it.

Sarah and Dave are relaxing at home.

Sarah: Would you .....*like*..... another cup of .....*coffee*....... ?

Dave: ...., thanks. I don't .... so.

Sarah: Is there anything .... in the .... ?

Dave: Well, there's something about a .... escape.

Sarah: Oh, really?

Dave: Yeah. A couple of .... escaped from the state prison in a .... van.

Sarah: Hmm . . . . we know .... with a minivan?

Dave: A minivan? What .... is it?

Sarah: I .... know. Light .... , maybe, or .... I can't .... very well.

Dave: Where is this .... ?

Sarah: It's parked right in .... of the .... And there are .... guys in it.

10 MODIFIERS WITH PARTICIPLES AND PREPOSITIONS

A Look at the picture. Match the information in columns A, B, and C.

A	B	C
Sarah	is the young one	holding his hat
Dave	is the heavy one	with glasses
George	is the blonde woman	wearing a green shirt
Don	is the bald man	wearing a blue T-shirt

B *Pair work* What else do you remember about the people in the video? Write at least three more sentences of your own.

1) ....   3) ....

2) ....

11 DESCRIBING SOMEONE

A *Pair work* Take turns asking and answering questions about a classmate. Try to guess who the person is.

A: Is it a tall person with short hair?
B: No, the person is short . . .

B Write five sentences describing your classmates. Two of your sentences should be false. Then read your sentences. Your partner says **True** or **False** and corrects the false sentences.

A: Steve's the tall guy wearing a blue shirt.
B: False. He's wearing a white shirt.

10 Sorry I'm late.

1 CULTURE

In the United States and Canada, people usually like others to be on time,
but for some occasions it's OK to be a little late.

For class or a business appointment,	**plan to arrive**	on time or a little early.
When you meet a friend,		on time or 5 to 10 minutes late.
When someone invites you to dinner,		about 10 to 15 minutes late.
For an informal party,		a little late (15 to 30 minutes).

Are people usually on time for appointments in your country?
Is it OK to arrive late when you meet a friend for dinner? When you
go to an informal party?

2 VOCABULARY Past tense of verbs

Pair work Do you know the past tense of these verbs? Complete the chart.

Present	Past	Present	Past
call	_called_	lock	
do		open	
find		pay	
get		remember	
go		send	
leave		start	

3 GUESS THE STORY

Watch the first minute of the video with the sound off.
What do you think happened? Check (✓) all correct answers.

- ☐ The man arrived very late for dinner.
- ☐ The woman was angry.
- ☐ The man didn't have his wallet.
- ☐ The woman paid for dinner.

44

 **Watch the video**

4 GET THE PICTURE

What really happened? Check (✓) the correct answers. Then compare with a partner.

1) What was the problem with Tom's car?
   - ☐ It didn't start.
   - ☐ He locked his keys in it.
   - ☐ He forgot to buy gasoline.

2) What was the problem with Tom's wallet?
   - ☐ He left it in the car.
   - ☐ He lost it.
   - ☐ He had no money in it.

3) Who paid for dinner?
   - ☐ Tom paid.
   - ☐ Marie paid.
   - ☐ Tom and Marie each paid half.

5 WATCH FOR DETAILS

A Put the pictures in order (1 to 6). Then write the correct sentence under each picture. Compare with a partner.

Tom remembered his wallet was in the house.
Tom tried to call Marie.
Tom called a lock service.

Tom remembered his wallet was in the car.
Tom saw his keys inside the car.
✓Tom left the house and started his car.

....
....

....
....

....
....

Tom left the house and
started his car.

....
....

....
....

B *Pair work* What else happened? Can you add two things?

1) ....

2) ....

6 WHAT'S YOUR OPINION?

Pair work Complete the chart. Check (✓) the words that describe
Tom and Marie.

	Angry	*Upset*	*Tired*	*Embarrassed*	*Understanding*	*Worried*
Tom	☐	☐	☐	☐	☐	☐
Marie	☐	☐	☐	☐	☐	☐

Follow-up

7 QUESTION GAME

A Write three more questions about the story. Use the past tense
and **how**, **why**, **how much**, **who**, or **where**.

1) *Why did Tom go back to his apartment?* ....
2) *When did Tom lock his keys in the car?* ....
3) ....
4) ....
5) ....

B **Pair work** Answer your partner's questions. If you don't think
the answer was in the video, say **It didn't say**.

8 TELL THE STORY

Pair work Write out the story using **first**, **after that**, **next**,
then, and **finally**. Include one mistake. Then read your story
to another pair. Can they find the mistake?

First, Tom left his apartment and started ....
....
....
....
....
....
....
....

Language close-up

9 WHAT DID THEY SAY?

Watch the video and complete the conversation. Then practice it.

Marie is waiting for Tom in the restaurant when he arrives late.

Marie: Hi. .....*There*...... will be ....*two*.... of us. . . . Thank you. . . .

Tom: Marie! I'm really .... How ....
have you been waiting?

Marie: It's ...., Tom. I've only .... here
for a little .... Is everything all .... ?

Tom: Yes, it is ...., but you won't .... what
just happened to ....

Marie: Well, what .... ?

Tom: Well, ... of all, I was a little ....
leaving my .... , and so I was in a
.... Then, just after I .... the car,
I .... I didn't have any ....
with me, so I went .... to get my ....

Marie: Did you .... it?

Tom: Oh, yes! I .... it. That wasn't the ....
The problem .... when I got .... to
my .... , I couldn't .... in.

Marie: Do you mean you .... your keys in the car?

Tom: That's .... So, guess what I did .... that!

Marie: I .... guess.

10 PRESENT PERFECT

A *Pair work* Write questions using **Have you ever . . . ?** and the correct
forms of the verbs in parentheses. Can you add three questions to the list?

1) *Have you ever locked* .... (lock) your keys in the car?
2) .... (call) a lock service?
3) .... (leave) your wallet in the car?
4) .... (arrive) late for an important dinner?
5) .... (go) to a restaurant without money?
6) .... (wait) a long time for someone in a restaurant?
7) ....
8) ....
9) ....

B *Class activity* Go around the class and interview at least three classmates.
Who answered "yes" to the most questions?

11 Across the Golden Gate Bridge

1 CULTURE

The city of San Francisco is surrounded by water on three sides. To the east, the Oakland Bay Bridge crosses San Francisco Bay to the city of Berkeley, home of the Berkeley campus of the University of California. To the north, visitors can see the famous Golden Gate Bridge. The first stop across this bridge is Sausalito, a beautiful town with shops and restaurants on the water. A short drive away is the redwood forest Muir Woods. It has some of the tallest trees in the world. Less than an hour away by car is the Napa Valley, famous for some of California's best wine.

Do you know any other places near San Francisco?
When you visit a city, do you use the bus or train, or do you rent a car?

2 VOCABULARY Taking a trip

Pair work Match the pictures with the words in the glossary below.

1) *winery*

2) ....

3) ....

4) ....

5) ....

6) ....

bay a wide opening of water that is an entrance to the sea
forest an area of land covered with trees
valley an area of land between two hills or mountains

vineyard a piece of land planted with grapes for making wine
waterfront part of a town near a sea or ocean
✓**winery** a factory that makes wine

48

3 GUESS THE STORY

Watch the video with the sound off. Where do you think the couple goes first?

1) Sausalito

2) The Napa Valley

3) Muir Woods

Watch the video

4 GET THE PICTURE

What places does the car-rental agent talk about? Circle them.
Then compare with a partner.

The Napa Valley   Oakland   Alcatraz Island

Sausalito   Muir Woods   The Golden Gate Bridge

5 WATCH FOR DETAILS

Why should the Changs go to the places below? Complete the sentences.
Then compare with a partner.

1) The _wineries_ and .... there are some of the most famous in California.

2) It's a fascinating little .... just across the ....

3) It's right on the .... , and there's a wonderful view of .... across the ....

4) It's a beautiful redwood ....

49

6 COMPLETE THE STORY

Complete the paragraph below. Choose words from the list. Then
compare with a partner.

Golden Gate	hungry	the Napa Valley	Sausalito	week
✓Honolulu	Muir Woods	rent	waterfront	wineries

The Changs arrive in San Francisco from ....Honolulu............. . They ....
a car at the airport for one .... because they plan to visit friends in
.... The rental agent tells them about the famous ....
there. They decide to drive across the .... Bridge and have lunch in
.... on the way.

Follow-up

7 SAN FRANCISCO

Group work Imagine you have two days in San Francisco. Plan your itinerary.

1) Decide which places you will go to each day.
2) Decide if you need a car.

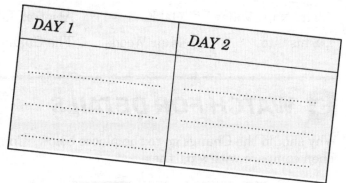

DAY 1	DAY 2
....	....
....	....
....	....

Ghirardelli Square

Golden Gate Park

Fisherman's Wharf

Muir Woods

Chinatown

Sausalito

8 YOUR CITY

A Group work Now imagine the Changs are
visiting your city. Plan their itinerary. Give at
least six suggestions like this:

A: First, I think they should drive to . . .
B: Yes, and they should also go to . . .

B Class activity Share your information
with the class.

Language close-up

9 WHAT DID THEY SAY?

Watch the video and complete the conversation. Then practice it.

The Changs are at the car-rental agency at the airport.

Ken: Good .... *morning* .... May I ....*help*..... you?

Mr. Chang: Yes, we're .... to pick up a ....

Ken: Do you .... a reservation?

Mr. Chang: Yes. The .... is Chang.

Ken: OK, Chang, Chang. Here it is, Mr. Chang.
              .... in advance. .... here and here.
              And that's for one .... then?

Mr. Chang: That's .... One week.

Ken: Are you .... in San Francisco?

Mrs. Chang: No, we're .... to visit ....
              in the Napa Valley.

Ken: Oh, Napa Valley. That's one of my ....
              places. The wineries and .... there are some
              of the most .... in California.

10 SHOULD *AND* SHOULDN'T *Giving advice*

A Complete these sentences with **should** or **shouldn't**. Then
compare with a partner

1) When you visit a foreign country, you ....*should*........ learn
   a few words of the local language.

2) You .... find out about the weather before you travel.

3) You .... carry a lot of cash when you travel.

4) You .... talk to a travel agent about interesting
   places to visit.

5) You .... be afraid to ask local people questions.

B *Pair work* Give advice for things visitors to your city should or
shouldn't do. Write three suggestions in each column.

They should . . .	*They shouldn't . . .*
1)	1) ....
2)	2) ....
3)	3) ....

12 Feeling bad

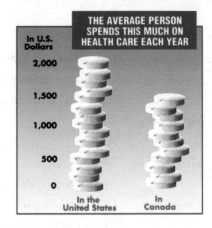
1 CULTURE

In the United States and Canada, people spend more on health care than in other parts of the world. In drugstores, people buy over-the-counter drugs for colds, coughs, and sore throats. In health-food stores, they buy vitamins and natural foods. Home remedies for common illnesses such as colds and sore throats are also popular.

In U.S. Dollars	THE AVERAGE PERSON SPENDS THIS MUCH ON HEALTH CARE EACH YEAR

Do you take vitamins or other food supplements?
Do you have health-food stores in your country? What do they sell?

2 VOCABULARY Cold remedies

Pair work Put the remedies in the chart. Can you add two more to each category?

aspirin

chicken soup

cough medicine

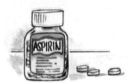

garlic juice

ginseng tea

tea with lemon

Home remedies		Over-the-counter drugs	
chicken soup			

52

3 GUESS THE STORY

Watch the video with the sound off. Answer these questions.

What's the man's problem?
Which remedies in Exercise 2 do you think his co-workers suggest?

 Watch the video

4 GET THE PICTURE

Check (✓) the correct answers. Compare them with a partner.

1) Sandy offers Steve
   - ☐ something she made.
   - ☐ something from the drugstore.
   - ☐ something from a health-food store.

2) Jim offers Steve
   - ☐ something he bought.
   - ☐ something his mother makes for him.
   - ☐ something from a health-food store.

3) Rebecca says Steve should
   - ☐ see the doctor.
   - ☐ take some more medicine.
   - ☐ go out to lunch.

5 WATCH FOR DETAILS

Check (✓) all correct answers. Then compare with a partner.

1) Sandy says her remedy
   - ☐ tastes bad.
   - ☐ contains ginseng.
   - ☐ makes you sleepy.

2) Jim says his remedy
   - ☐ is great for a cold.
   - ☐ makes you sleepy.
   - ☐ has garlic, onions, and carrots in it.

3) Rebecca says her remedy
   - ☐ is the best cure of all.
   - ☐ can be made at home.
   - ☐ mixes with water.

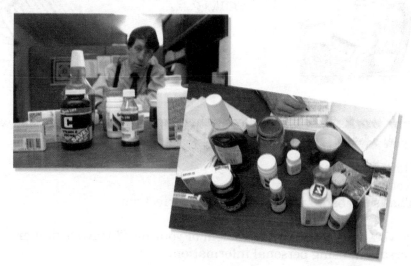

6 WHAT'S YOUR OPINION?

Pair work Answer these questions.

1) Which remedy does Steve like best?
2) Which remedy do you think is best for Steve's cold?
3) Do you think Steve should be at work today?

 *Follow-up*

7 HEALTH PROBLEMS

A ***Group work*** What do you do for these problems? Can you add two more remedies for each? Compare around the class. Who has the best remedies?

1) a bad cold
   It's a good idea to stay in bed and rest. Try some . . . .

2) a cough
   You should drink hot tea. It's important to . . . .

3) a headache
   Take some aspirin. It's helpful to . . . .

4) a backache
   You should lie on the floor. Get some . . . .

B ***Pair work*** Take turns playing the role of Steve. Your partner will give you advice.

A: How do you feel?
B: Not too good. I've got . . .
A: That's too bad. Listen. I've got the perfect cure . . .

C Do you need advice for a problem of your own? Have a similar conversation, using personal information.

Language close-up

8 WHAT DID THEY SAY?

Watch the video and complete the conversation. Then practice it.

Steve is at work with a bad cold when Sandy comes in.

Sandy: How are those _____papers_____ coming for this _____afternoon_____, Steve?
Steve: _____ finished.
Sandy: Do you _____ have that _____?
Steve: Yeah, _____ still pretty _____, Sandy.
Sandy: Listen, I've _____ just the _____ for you. Just a _____ . . . . Here.
Steve: What's _____?
Sandy: It's _____ I picked up at the _____-food store. You just mix it with _____ water and _____ it.
Steve: But _____ is it?
Sandy: I'm not really _____. I think it _____ ginseng in it or something _____ that. Try it.
Steve: Are you sure it _____?
Sandy: Of _____ it does.
Steve: Well, _____, Sandy. That's really _____. Maybe later.

9 REQUESTS AND SUGGESTIONS

A Complete the conversations with **may** or **could** to make requests and **should**, **try**, or **suggest** to give suggestions. Then compare and practice with a partner.

1) *At the office*

A: Here's the perfect cold medicine: garlic juice, onions, and carrots. You _____should_____ drink a cup every two hours.
B: But I don't like carrots.
A: Well, then I _____ an old-fashioned bowl of chicken soup! And _____ to get some rest, too.

I HAVE THE PERFECT CURE FOR YOU.

2) *At a pharmacy*

A: _____ I help you?
B: Yes. _____ I have something good for a cold? It's a bad one.
A: Yes. I have these pills. They're a little strong. Just don't drive after you take them.
B: Hmm . . . I drive to work. _____ I have something else?
A: Well, _____ these other pills then. They won't make you sleepy.

B *Pair work* Act out the conversations. The first time, act them out as is. The second time, change the problems and the remedies.

At the Mall of America

Preview

1 CULTURE

The Mall of America is the largest shopping and entertainment mall in the United States. It takes up 4.2 million square feet (or 390,000 square meters) of space. In addition to four major department stores, you can find almost 400 other stores, an entertainment park with 50 rides, over 30 restaurants, a movie theater with 14 screens, and numerous live music clubs. Built in 1990, the mall is still very new. The original idea for the mall came from the Triple Five Corporation, a Canadian company that built the largest shopping mall in the world in West Edmonton, Alberta.

Are shopping malls popular in your country?
What do you think are the advantages of shopping at a mall?
  The disadvantages?

Watch the video

2 GET THE PICTURE

Check (✓) the correct answers. Then compare with a partner.

1) The Mall of America is in
   ☐ Bloomington, Indiana.
   ☑ Bloomington, Minnesota.

2) The mall has
   ☐ hundreds of stores.
   ☐ thousands of stores.

3) There are
   ☐ 14 cinemas.
   ☐ 40 cinemas.

4) There are more than
   ☐ 14 places to eat.
   ☐ 40 places to eat.

5) The name of the amusement park is
   ☐ Camp Winnie.
   ☐ Camp Snoopy.

3 WATCH FOR DETAILS

What did these people do at the mall? Check (✓) all true answers. Then compare with a partner.

1) ☐ She went to Camp Snoopy.
   ☐ She bought some shoes.
   ☐ She ate lunch.

2) ☐ They went on rides.
   ☐ They looked in stores.
   ☐ They ate lunch.

3) ☐ They listened to music.
   ☐ They bought some tapes.
   ☐ They went to Camp Snoopy.

4 WHAT THE SHOPPERS SAY

How did these people answer the reporter's questions? Fill in the blanks. Then compare with a partner.

1) What do you think people should do first?

2) What would you recommend for visitors from another country?

3) Can you describe the Mall of America in one word?

  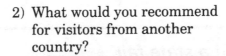

Wear .... shoes.

Come here if there's anything
.... you're
looking for.

....

 **Follow-up**

5 WHAT'S YOUR OPINION?

Pair work Answer these questions.

1) Do you like shopping malls?
2) How would you describe the Mall of America?
3) What places would you like to visit at the mall?

13 At the state fair

1 CULTURE

In rural areas of the United States and Canada, where farming is important, a state or county fair is a popular summer event. At the fair, farmers show their fruits and vegetables, their best animals, and their new equipment. There are competitions such as horseback riding and rodeos. People sell paintings and handmade products such as pottery. There are rides and games for the entire family. And there are always lots of things to eat. For young children, a day at the fair is one of the happiest days of the year.

Do you have fairs in your country? What kind? What can you do and see there?
Where can families go in your country to have fun together?

2 VOCABULARY At a state fair

Pair work Here are some things you can do at a state fair. Write the activities under the pictures.

eat corn on the cob   ride a horse   ride on a roller coaster
eat ice cream   ride on a merry-go-round   ✓win a prize

1) *win a prize*

2) ....

3) ....

4) ....

5) ....

6) ....

3 GUESS THE STORY

Who do you think wins the prize? Check (✓) your answer.

☐ Rick

☐ Betsy

☐ Nancy

  Watch the video

4 GET THE PICTURE

What did each group of people do? Check (✓) all correct answers.
Then compare with a partner.

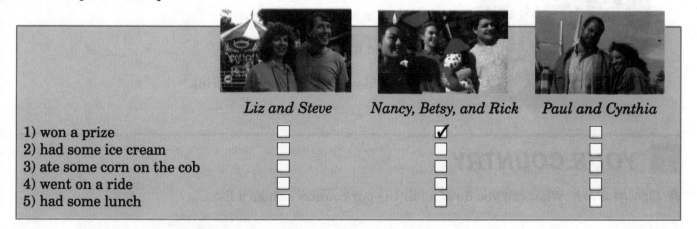

	Liz and Steve	Nancy, Betsy, and Rick	Paul and Cynthia
1) won a prize	☐	✓	☐
2) had some ice cream	☐	☐	☐
3) ate some corn on the cob	☐	☐	☐
4) went on a ride	☐	☐	☐
5) had some lunch	☐	☐	☐

5 WATCH FOR DETAILS

A List the things to do, eat, and see at a state fair. Then combine
answers as a class and complete the chart.

Things to do	Things to eat	Things to see
ride a horse		

B Which of these things have you done? Check (✓) them.
Then compare with a partner.

6 *A DAY AT THE FAIR*

A *Group work* Plan a day at the state fair in the video. Agree on five things to do and see.

1) ....

2) ....

3) ....

4) ....

5) ....

B *Pair work* Order lunch at the state fair. One student will play the waiter or waitress.

A: May I take your order, please?
B: . . .
A: Would you like anything else?
B: . . .
A: And would you like anything to drink?
B: . . .

7 *YOUR COUNTRY*

A *Group work* What can you do at a fair in your country? Make a list.

Things to do	Things to eat	Things to see
....	....	....
....	....	....
....	....	....
....	....	....

B Which things are your favorite? Check (✓) at least three. Then have conversations like this:

A: I like to go on rides.
B: I like to play games and try to win prizes.

C In the United States, corn on the cob is very popular. What foods are popular where you're from?

Language close-up

8 WHAT DID THEY SAY?

Watch the video and complete the conversations. Then practice them.

Some people are enjoying a day at the state fair.

1) Vendor: Hey, this is the ....*place*...... ! Get your fresh corn on
the .... here! Fresh, ...-roasted ....
on the cob! . . . What .... you like?

   Steve: I'll .... one of .... , please.

   Vendor: Coming .... What about .... ? Would you
   .... one, too?

   Liz: Not right .... , thank you. I'm not ....

   Steve: Maybe you .... give us another .... anyway!

   Vendor: Sure.

2) Nancy: Oh, he is *so* .... !

   Rick: Yeah, but that .... a lot of .... Now let's .... a
   place to ....

   Betsy: How about over .... ? There's a ....
   where we can .... down, too. My .... are tired.

   Waitress: Hi! .... I take your .... ?

   Betsy: Yeah, I .... I'll have a hot .... and a small ....
   of french fries.

   Waitress: Would you .... anything to .... ?

   Betsy: I'll have a .... diet cola.

   Waitress: OK. And .... can I .... for you?

   Nancy: I guess .... like the .... plate and a cup of .... , please.

9 WOULD AND WILL Ordering food

A Rewrite these questions using **Would you like . . . ?**
Then compare with a partner.

1) What do you want to eat?
   What would you like to eat?

2) Do you want french fries with that?

   ....

3) Do you want dessert?

   ....

4) Do you want anything to drink?

   ....

B *Pair work* Now answer the questions with **I'll have . . .**

A: What would you like to eat?
B: I'll have . . .

61

Preview

1 CULTURE

One of the most popular TV programs in the United States and Canada is the game show. In most game shows, players test their knowledge on different subjects, and the questions are sometimes difficult. But there are also game shows that are games of chance. The winner must be lucky, but doesn't have to be smart. And there are even dating "game shows." The prize isn't money, but a chance to meet someone new!

Do you have game shows on TV in your country?
What kinds of game shows are popular?

POPULAR TV

JEOPARDY
A Game of Knowledge
Love Connection
A Dating Game
Wheel of Fortune
A Game of Chance

GAME SHOWS IN THE U.S.

2 GUESS THE FACTS

Pair work How good is your geography?
Check the correct answers.

1) Which is longer?
   □ the Nile River
   □ the Amazon River

the Amazon River

2) Which is higher?
   □ Mt. McKinley
   □ Mt. Kilimanjaro

the Nile River

3) Which country is called the "island continent"?
   □ New Zealand
   □ Australia

Mt. McKinley

Mt. Kilimanjaro

4) What's the largest desert in Asia?
   ☐ the Great Indian desert
   ☐ the Gobi desert

Los Angeles

Mexico City

5) Which is the largest city in
   North America?
   ☐ Los Angeles
   ☐ Mexico City

6) Where is Angel Falls, the
   world's highest waterfall?
   ☐ Brazil
   ☐ Venezuela

Angel Falls

 **Watch the video**

3 CHECK THE FACTS

Now correct your answers to Exercise 2. Did you guess the facts
correctly? Compare with a partner.

4 WATCH FOR DETAILS

Check (✓) the correct answers. Then compare with a partner.

1) Marlene is from
   ☐ Seattle, Washington.
   ☐ Washington, D.C.

2) Marlene is a
   ☐ computer programmer.
   ☐ computer engineer.

3) Jack is from
   ☐ Cambridge, Massachusetts.
   ☐ Boston, Massachusetts.

4) Jack is a
   ☐ high school teacher.
   ☐ college teacher.

5) Kathy is from
   ☐ Vero Beach, Florida.
   ☐ Miami Beach, Florida.

6) Kathy is an
   ☐ actress.
   ☐ accountant.

5 WHO WINS THE GAME?

A What is each person's score at the end of the game? Write the number. Then compare with a partner.

Marlene ....   Jack ....   Kathy ....

B Is the winner happy with the prize? Why or why not?

Follow-up

6 AROUND THE WORLD

A *Group work* Write questions for the game "Around the World." Write three questions for each category in the chart. Give one question 25 points, one question 50 points, and one question 75 points. (You can also add categories of your own.)

Deserts and mountains	Oceans and islands
....	....
....	....
....	....
Rivers and waterfalls	Cities and countries
....	....
....	....
....	....

B *Class activity* Now play "Around the World." Half the class is in Group A. The other half is in Group B.

Group A: Choose one student to be the game-show host.

Group B: Take turns choosing a category for 25, 50, or 75 points. Then answer the host's questions. Play for five minutes.

Ask questions like this:

A: Are you ready?
B: Yes, I'll try (*name of category*) for 25 points.
A: OK. (*Asks question.*)
B: (*Answers question.*)
A: That's right! **or** Sorry. That's not correct.

Now change roles. Group B chooses a host and Group A answers questions. Play for five more minutes. Which group wins the game?

Language close-up

7 WHAT DID THEY SAY?

Watch the video and complete the conversation. Then practice it.

Marlene, Jack, and Kathy are about to begin playing "Around the World."

Announcer: And now it's ....time.... to play "Around the ....World.... "
with your host, Johnny Traveler.

Johnny: .... and gentlemen, ... to
"Around the World," the .... show about world
.... And now, let's .... our players.

Announcer: A .... engineer from .... ,
Washington, Marlene Miller! A high ....
teacher from .... , Massachusetts, Jack
Richardson! And from Vero Beach, Florida, an
.... , Kathy Hernandez!

Johnny: .... to "Around the World." And now, let's
.... our game. Our categories are ....
and Mountains, ... and Waterfalls, Oceans and
.... , Cities and .... Marlene, please begin.

8 COMPARISONS WITH ADJECTIVES

A Write questions using the comparative or superlative form of each
adjective in parentheses. Then add three questions of your own.

1) city: New York – Tokyo? (cold)
   Which city is colder, New York or Tokyo?

2) planet: Earth – Saturn – Mars? (big)
   ....

3) plane: the Concorde – a 747? (fast)
   ....

4) building: the Parthenon – the Empire State
   Building? (old)
   ....

5) country: Brazil – Canada – Argentina? (large)
   ....

6) ....

7) ....

8) ....

New York is colder!

B *Pair work* Take turns asking and answering the questions.
Who answered the most questions correctly?

15 May I speak to Cathy?

Preview

1 CULTURE

In the United States and Canada, people like to talk on the telephone. In many places, the cost of a local call is fixed. You can talk for five minutes or two hours for the same price. The telephone is now very convenient because of new technology. Here are some examples:

- *Call waiting* – You can answer a second call when you are on the telephone.
- *Call forwarding* – You can receive telephone calls at a different phone number.
- *Answering machines* – You don't miss calls when you're busy or not at home.
- *Cellular phones* – You can make and receive telephone calls in your car.
- *Two telephone lines on one phone* – Different rings tell you who the call is for.

How much time do you spend on the telephone each day?
What kinds of new technology are common in your country?
 Which do you like best?

2 VOCABULARY Telephone expressions

A *Pair work* Match.

...c..... 1) Cathy's not here right now.
.... 2) May I speak to Cathy?
.... 3) She's not in just now.
.... 4) Will she be back soon?
.... 5) Could you tell her that Kevin called?
.... 6) Is she coming back soon?
.... 7) Is Cathy home?
.... 8) Could you just tell her to call me?

a) Asking to speak to someone
b) Leaving a message
c) Saying someone is out
d) Asking for information about someone

B Can you add three other telephone expressions?

1) ....

2) ....

3) ....

3 GUESS THE STORY

Watch the first two minutes of the video with the sound off.
What do you think these people are saying? Write one sentence from
Exercise 2 in each balloon.

Kevin

May I speak to Cathy?

Mr. Waite

Mr. Waite

Jenny

Watch the video

4 GET THE PICTURE

A Put the phone calls in order. Number them from 1 to 3. Then compare with a partner.

Kevin

Rachel

Jenny

B Complete the telephone messages for Cathy. Fill in the names of the callers
and check the correct messages. Then compare with a partner.

1) .... called.
   ☐ will call Cathy back
   ☐ wants Cathy to call

2) .... called.
   ☐ will call Cathy back
   ☐ wants Cathy to call

3) .... called.
   ☐ will call Cathy back
   ☐ wants Cathy to call

5 TELEPHONE ETIQUETTE

A When you make a phone call, it's polite to give your name. What does each person say when Mr. Waite answers the phone? Fill in the balloons. Then compare with a partner.

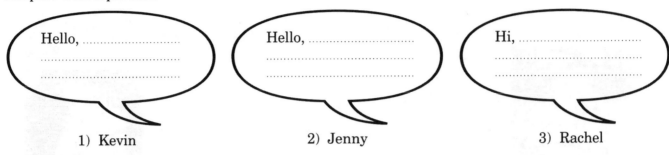

Hello, ...

1) Kevin

Hello, ...

2) Jenny

Hi, ...

3) Rachel

B *Pair work* Who do you think is the most polite? Why?

6 WHAT'S YOUR OPINION?

Pair work Look at the culture preview again. Which telephone conveniences do you think Mr. Waite needs? Give each a number from 1 to 5 (1 = most useful).

Follow-up

7 FINISH THE STORY

A *Pair work* What do you think Mr. Waite says to his boss? What do you think the urgent call was about? Write a possible telephone conversation.

Start like this:

Mr. Waite: John speaking.
Boss: I'm very sorry to bother you, John. I hope it's not a problem.
Mr. Waite: Oh no, no! Uh, no problem! No problem at all!
Boss: I'm calling because . . .
Mr. Waite: . . .

B *Class activity* Practice your conversations in front of the class. Who has the best conversation?

Language close-up

8 *WHAT DID THEY SAY?*

Watch the video and complete the conversations. Then practice them.

Cathy's father is home alone when the phone rings.

1) Mr. Waite: Hello?
   Kevin: Hello, ..*may*.. I speak ..*to*.. Cathy?
   Mr. Waite: I'm .... She's not .... just now.
   Kevin: Is she .... back soon?
   Mr. Waite: Uh, ..., I think ....
   Kevin: Well, ... you tell .... that
              Kevin .... and that I'll call .... later?
   Mr. Waite: ...., Kevin.
   Kevin: .... you. Good-bye.
   Mr. Waite: Bye.

2) Mr. Waite: Hello?
   Jenny: .... , Mr. Waite. .... is Jenny. Is
              Cathy .... ?
   Mr. Waite: Oh, hi, Jenny. No, Cathy's .... here
              right ....
   Jenny: .... she be .... soon?
   Mr. Waite: Uh, I'm not .... Would you ....
              to leave a .... ?
   Jenny: Well, ... you just .... her to call ....
              when she .... in?
   Mr. Waite: Sure, ... tell her. .... , Jenny.
   Jenny: Bye, ... Waite.

3) Mr. Waite: Hello?
   Rachel: .... , this is Rachel. .... Cathy home?
   Mr. Waite: Uh, no, she's .... , Rachel. .... you like
              her to .... you .... she comes .... ?
   Rachel: Yes, ... She has my ....
   Mr. Waite: I'll .... her, Rachel. Bye.
   Rachel: Bye.

9 *REQUESTS WITH TELL AND ASK*

Pair work Practice the conversations in Exercise 8 again.
This time use your own information and make requests with
ask or **tell** like this:

Would you tell Cathy the party is at Kevin's house?
Could you ask Cathy to meet us at Burger Heaven at 2:00?

16 A whole new Marty

 **Preview**

1 CULTURE

Self-improvement is an important part of Canadian and American cultures. Many people believe that life will be better for them if they change their appearance in some way. Magazines and newspapers often have advertisements for exercise machines, vitamins, skin and hair products, and courses on self-improvement. Among young people, a good appearance is usually important, and so is the ability to make friends easily.

Is self-improvement an important part of your culture?
Do you want to change anything about yourself?

3 Steps to a Better You

1 Exercise bicycle $119.95

2 Self-help book $19.95 — I Love Me

3 Super vitamins $39.95

TO ORDER, CALL 800-555-3210

2 VOCABULARY Verb and noun pairs

Pair work Choose a verb from the list to go with each word or phrase. (Some items have more than one answer.)

buy   cut   gain   ✓improve   make
✓change   do   get   lose   meet

1) *change or improve* my appearance		6)		some new clothes
2) .... more people		7)		my hairstyle
3) .... more friends		8)		my hair
4) .... weight		9)		in shape
5) .... more exercise		10)		confidence

3 GUESS THE STORY

Watch the first minute of the video with the sound off.
Check (✓) the phrases you think describe each person.

	Marty	John
1) looks unhappy	☐	☐
2) is popular with girls	☐	☐
3) dresses well	☐	☐
4) has trouble with a calculus problem	☐	☐

Marty

John

Watch the video

4 GET THE PICTURE

A Check your answers to Exercise 3. Did you guess correctly?

B Check (✓) **True** or **False**. Correct the false statements. Then compare with a partner.

Marty

John

Michelle

	True	False	
1) John asks Marty for help with his schoolwork.	☐	☐	....
2) Michelle doesn't know Marty.	☐	☐	....
3) Michelle and John decide to study calculus together.	☐	☐	....
4) John thinks Marty should be more outgoing.	☐	☐	....
5) Michelle recognizes Marty in the cafeteria.	☐	☐	....
6) Marty is too busy to study with Michelle.	☐	☐	....

5 WATCH FOR DETAILS

Check (✓) the things Marty does to improve his appearance.

☐ He lifts weights.

☐ He gets a haircut.

☐ He changes his diet.

☐ He buys new clothes.

☐ He shaves.

☐ He takes vitamins.

Follow-up

6 WHAT HAPPENED?

A Write the story in your own words.

1) .John and Marty were.   2) ....   3) ....
    .in the library.   ....

4) ....   5) ....   6) ....
    ....

B *Pair work* Now share your description of what happened with
a partner. How are your stories different?

7 GOOD ADVICE

What advice would you give to these people? Think of as many things
as you can for each person.

1) Maria has trouble meeting boys.
2) Tina has trouble with math.
3) Tony is shy.
4) Karen wants to get in shape.

> He could . . .
> She should . . .
> It's important/helpful/useful/a good idea to . . .

Language close-up

8 WHAT DID THEY SAY?

Watch the video and complete the conversation. Then practice it.

John and Marty are in the library when Michelle comes by.

John: I'm just ...terrible... at calculus. I don't ....
anything in this ....

Marty: I .... what you .... It is a .... course.

John: Did you .... out the answer to this .... ?

Marty: That's in Chapter 11. I .... that .... week. Let's see.

Michelle: Hi, John. I .... you're .... on calculus.

John: Oh, hi, Michelle. Yes, I .... Michelle, you .... Marty,
.... you?

Michelle: Yeah, hi, Marty. Say, John, I've got a .... of
.... about Chapter 12. Do you want to
.... together?

John: Well, uh, actually, I'm .... on Chapter 11, but Marty
.... is working on Chapter 12.

Michelle: Oh, that's OK. Actually, I've .... go to class
.... now. See you ....

John: OK, Michelle. ....

9 DESCRIBING CHANGES

A Complete the sentences with the correct form of each word.
Then compare with a partner.

busy	buy	change	drive
long	paint	start	wear

1) I .... glasses now.

2) I don't .... to work anymore. I take the bus.

3) I haven't cut my hair in four months. It's .... than before.

4) I got a promotion at work recently. I'm much .... now.

5) I .... my bedroom blue last weekend.

6) I .... a new computer course last week.

7) I've .... a dog.

8) I've .... my hairstyle.

B Now write four similar sentences about yourself and read them to your partner.
Who has changed more in the past year?

1) ....

2) ....

3) ....

4) ....

What is American food?

1 CULTURE

Many people think American food is just hot dogs and pizza. Of course, these things are popular, but even in small towns in the United States, you can find Chinese, Italian, and Mexican restaurants. In many places there are Japanese, Thai, and German restaurants. The United States is a country of immigrants, and there are as many kinds of food as there are people from different backgrounds.

What foods are typical of your country or region?
What is your favorite food?

Watch the video

2 GET THE PICTURE

In the video, in what kind of restaurant can you find these foods?
Write **CA** for California style, **A** for American, **C** for Chinese,
or **G** for German.

1) bratwurst

2) Caesar salad

3) a hamburger

4) Kung-pao chicken

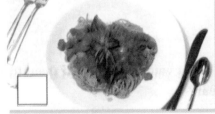

5) pasta

6) pork Szechwan

3 WATCH FOR DETAILS

Match the people with what they ate. Choose foods
from the list. Then compare with a partner.

Bavarian goulash   Caesar salad   German potato salad   pasta
bratwurst   chicken salad   Kung-pao chicken   pork Szechwan

1) ....

2) ....

3) ....

4) ....

5) ....

6) ....

4 IT'S ALL AMERICAN FOOD

Answer the questions. Then compare with a partner.

1) California-style restaurants are famous for
   their interesting use of
   ☐ fresh fish.
   ☐ pasta.
   ☑ fresh fruits and vegetables.

2) The Chinese restaurant has
   ☐ food with live music.
   ☐ a self-service buffet.
   ☐ vegetarian food.

3) In the German restaurant people can
   ☐ listen to music and eat.
   ☐ cook their own food.
   ☐ order a hamburger.

4) Most people in the video think typical
   American food is
   ☐ steak.
   ☐ a hamburger and french fries.
   ☐ barbecue.

 *Follow-up*

5 HOW ABOUT YOU?

Group work Answer these questions.

1) What does the reporter say American food is?
   What is American food to you?
2) How often do you eat out in restaurants?

3) What's your favorite kind of restaurant?
4) What do you usually order?
5) What's your favorite American food?

Acknowledgments

Illustrators

Adventure House 6 (*top*), 12 (*top*), 16, 18, 26 (*top*), 34 (*all*), 37, 48 (*top*), 52 (*top*), 62, 70
Brian Battles 12 (*bottom*), 14 (*bottom*)
Keith Bendis 2, 8, 10, 26 (*bottom*), 30, 42, 54, 66, 71
Mark Kaufman 48 (*bottom*), 58 (*top*)
Wally Neibart 4, 14 (*top*), 22 (*top*), 27, 36, 52 (*bottom*), 58 (*bottom*), 65
Andrew Toos 6 (*bottom*), 22 (*bottom*), 28, 39, 40, 44, 55, 61
Sam Viviano 24

Photographic Credits

49 (*top left*) © Bill Dean
62 (*clockwise from top left*) © Richard Steedman/The Stock Market; © Claudia Parks/The Stock Market; © Harvey Lloyd/The Stock Market; © Tom Bean/ The Stock Market
63 (*top; clockwise from top left*) © Pete Saloutos/The Stock Market; © Nigel Atherton/Tony Stone Worldwide; © Rob Crandall/Stock Boston

All other photographs by Rick Armstrong and John Hruska

Author's Acknowledgments

A great number of people assisted in the development of both the original *Interchange* Video 1 and *New Interchange* Video 1. Particular thanks go to the following:

The **reviewers** for their helpful suggestions:

Valerie A. Benson, Julie Dyson, Dorien Grunbaum, Cynthia Hall Kouré, Mark Kunce, Peter Mallett, Pamela Rogerson-Revell, Chuck Sandy, and Jody Simmons.

The **students** and **teachers** in the following schools and institutes who pilot-tested the Video or the Video Activity Book; their valuable comments and suggestions helped shape the content of the entire program:

Athenée Français, Tokyo, Japan; **Centro Cultural Brasil-Estados Unidos**, Belém, Brazil; **Eurocentres**, Virginia, U.S.A.; **Fairmont State College**, West Virginia, U.S.A.; **Hakodate Daigaku**, Hokkaido, Japan; **Hirosaki Gakuin Daigaku**, Aomori, Japan; **Hiroshima Shudo Daigaku**, Hiroshima, Japan; **Hokkaido Daigaku, Institute of Language and Cultural Studies**, Hokkaido, Japan; **The Institute Meguro**, Tokyo, Japan; **Instituto Brasil-Estados Unidos**, Rio de Janeiro, Brazil; **Instituto Cultural de Idiomas**, Caxias do Sul, Brazil; **Musashino Joshi Daigaku**, Tokyo, Japan; **Nagasaki Gaigo Tanki Daigaku**, Nagasaki, Japan; **New Cida**, Tokyo, Japan; **Parco-ILC English School**, Chiba, Japan; **Pegasus Language Services**, Tokyo, Japan; **Poole Gakuin Tanki Daigaku**, Hyogo, Japan; **Seinan Gakuin Daigaku**, Fukuoka, Japan; **Shukugawa Joshi Tanki Daigaku**, Hyogo, Japan; **Tokai Daigaku**, Kanagawa, Japan; **YMCA Business School**, Kanagawa, Japan; and **Yokohama YMCA**, Kanagawa, Japan.

The **editorial** and **production** team on the original or revised classroom video and the accompanying print materials:

Sarah Almy, Suzette André, John Borrelli, Will Capel, Mary Carson, Karen Davy, Andrew Gitzy, Deborah Goldblatt, Deborah Gordon, Stephanie Karras, James Morgan, Kathy Niemczyk, Chuck Sandy, Kathleen Schultz, Ellen Shaw, and Mary Vaughn.

The **editorial** and **production** team on *New Interchange* Level One: Suzette André, Sylvia P. Bloch, John Borrelli, Mary Carson, Natalie Nordby Chen, Karen Davy, Randee Falk, Andrew Gitzy, Pauline Ireland, Penny Laporte, Kathy Niemczyk, Kathleen Schultz, Rosie Stamp, and Mary Vaughn.

And Cambridge University Press **staff** and **advisors**: Carlos Barbisan, Kate Cory-Wright, Riitta da Costa, Peter Davison, Stephen Dawson, Peter Donovan, Cecilia Gómez, Colin Hayes, Thares Keeree, Jinsook Kim, Koen Van Landeghem, Carine Mitchell, Sabina Sahni, Helen Sandiford, Dan Schulte, Ian Sutherland, Chris White, and Ellen Zlotnick.

And a special thanks to the video producer, Master Communications Group.

1 First day at class

Rick starts at a university and gets a surprise .

Marie : I'm sorry , Miss Tanaka . What's your first Name again?

Sachiko : Sachiko . S-A-C-H-I-K-O.

Marie : Thanks . See you in a minute .

Rick : Hi . My name's Ricardo , but every body calls Me Rick .

Marie : Well nice to meet you, Rick .I'm Marie Ouellette.

Rick : It's nice to meet you , Marie .... Um , where Are you from . Marie?

Marie : I'm from Canada.

Rick : Oh , So you're Canadian ?

Marie : That's right .

Rick : From what city?

Marie : Montreal . How about you ?

Rick : I'm originally from Mexico City , but my Family and I live up here now .

Marie : Oh, are you a student here ?

Rick : Yes , I am .

Marie : what are you studying ?

Rick :Business Management ?

Marie : Oh , really! That's nice .

Rick : So, how about you ? Are you a student , too?

Marie : Well , no ,....

Rick : So, what do you do ?

Marie : I teach .

Rick : Oh ? what do you teach ?

Marie : Business Management .

=========

Sachiko : Excuse me , Miss Ouellette . This is our Classroom , isn't it ?

Marie : Yes , Sachiko , it is . Nice to meet you , Rick . Bye - bye!

Rick : Yeah , you too! Good –bye .

2 I need a change!

Lynn dreams about a new career.

Paula: Hi, Lynn! How are you doing?

Lynn: Oh, hi, Paula. Pretty good, thanks. How are you?

Paula: Not bad. Say, you know Bob Wallace, don't you?

Lynn: Oh, no, I don't think so. Hi, I'm Lynn Parker.

Bob: Pleased to meet you.

Paula: So, how's everything?

Lynn: Do you really want to know?

Paula: Of course I do.

Lynn: Well, it's my job.

Paula: But you have a great job.

Bob: Where do you work, Lynn?

Lynn: At AdTech.

Bob: what kind of business is that?

Lynn: It's a computer software company.

Bob: So, what do you do?

Lynn: I'm a manager in customer service.

Bob: Well, that sounds interesting.

Lynn: Well, . . . it is, but I'm at the office ten hours a day, six days a week. I'm always on the phone or at the computer. I need a change.

Paula: Well, what do you want to do, Lynn'?

Lynn: Actually, I want to work in a hotel.

Paula: A hotel'?

Lynn: In fact, I'm studying hotel management.

Paula: Really?

Lynn: Yes, I take evening: classes.

Paula: Well, that's great'

Lynn: And when I finish, I want to find a job in a warm climate.

Bob: You do? How about a job in Hawaii?

Lynn: Hawaii?

Bob: Sure. I have a friend who manages a hotel in Honolulu.

Lynn: Really?

Bob: Yeah. Maybe he has a job for you.

Paula: Hawaii ... well, that sounds great.... Oh, excuse me, I've got to get back to work.

Lynn: Oh. OK, Paula. Bye

Bob: Take it easy, Paula.

Paula: See you later.

Lynn: Hawaii ...

Jobs

People talk about what they do as we watch them at work

Reporter: Hi. I'm Mike Sullivan for KNOW News Seven. This is the Minneapolis Skyway. People use these skyways to go to and from their jobs. Now, let's go to where they work and see what kinds of jobs they have.

Architect: Hi. My name's Rob Reis. and I'm an architect.

Lawyer: Hi. I'm Laurie Peterson, and I'm a lawyer.

Pianist: Hello. My name is Vladimir Lavitsky, and I'm the pianist of the Minnesota Orchestra.

Computer engineer: Hi. I'm Pete ketchum, and I'm a computer engineer.

Cashier: Hi. My name is Cookie. I'm a part-time cashier at Byerly's.

Bank teller: Hi. I'm Shannon Bruin, and I'm a bank teller

Doctor: Hello. My name is Dr. Mari Eto. I work in an emergency room.

Chef: Hi. My name is James Williams, and I'm a chef. It's a great job, and I love it.

Photographer: Hi. M y name's Rick Armstrong, and I'm a commercial Photographer. Welcome to my Studio. ... I photograph people and things. .Mainly, I photograph people for magazines, and I photograph famous people for interviews . I enjoy meeting people.....I also take pictures of things advertisements' like shampoo and soap...
It's exciting job; there's something different everyday. But it's really hard work.
...Sometimes to get a good picture. I have to take fifty or sixty different shot,s of' exactly the same thing. It's certainly a challenge.

Travel-agency owner: Hello. I'm Sylvia Davis. I own Worldwide Travel. We plan tours to more than fifty different countries, and sometime I spend all day talking on the phone and writing faxes. . . . We're a small business with only three travel agents, so it's very busy here. A business is a big responsibility, but I get to travel, too. Several times a year my travel agents and 1 go to different, countries to look at now hotels. I love to travel' It's interesting and always different. How about you, do You like your job?

Reporter: Those are a few of the interesting jobs people have her in Minneapolis .This is Mike Sullivan for KNOW News Seven.

3 At a garage sale

Fred and Susan have different opinions about things at a garage sale.

Fred: Hey, Susan, how do you like this?
Susan: oh, please, Fred.
Fred: oh come on. It's only a dollar!
Susan: Do you really want it, Fred?
Fred: No, I guess you're right.

Vendor: Can I help you'?
Fred: No, thanks anyway. We re just looking.
Susan: oh. Fred, come over here. Just look at this lovely, old necklace!
Fred: Yeah, it's ok
Susan: It's not just ok, Fred. It's very nice! ... And look at this bracelet. Excuse me, how much are these ?
Vendor: oh, let's see. How about fifteen dollars for the two of them?
Fred: oh, that's not bad.
Susan: And how much is that old watch ?
Vendor: This one? oh, this one is, uh, twenty-five dollars.

Fred: Susan, are you kidding? Twenty-five dollars for that old watch'?
Vendor: This watch is old, but it still runs. Listen!
Susan: How old is it?
Vendor: oh, I don't really know. But it's very old.
Susan: oh, it is lovely.... I'll take it.
Fred: ok!
Vendor: Do you want those, too?
Susan: Yes, I'll take these, too.
Vendor's husband: Marge, is that my mother's watch?
Vendor: What? ... I don't know!
Vendor's husband: It is my mother's watch! Excuse me, but this watch is not for sale. I'm sorry.... Marge, could you come over here, please? *(to Fred and Susan)* I'm sorry.

Fred: Hey, Susan, look at this!

Susan: Oh, no, Fred. Not the motorcycle!

4 What kind of movies do you like?

Bill, Alfredo, and pat try to agree on what they should do one evening.

Bill: So,... what do we do now?
Alfredo: what time is it?
Bill: seven o'clock.
Pat: look , we all like movies . Why don't we rent a video and watch it at my house?
Bill: That's not a bad idea, pat.
Alfredo: its OK with me.
Bill: That's not a bad idea, pat.
Alfredo: it's ok with me.
Pat: well, then, come on! .... Now here are some great science- fiction movies! What do you think , Bill?
Bill: Uh I Cant stand sci-fi. How about a good suspense thriller?
Pat: Uh... Alfredo, what about you ? what do you think of science fiction.
Alfredo: Oh its o'k.
Bill: well, what kind of movies do you like?
Alfredo: I really like classic films a lot.
Pat: Then come over here. There are some great old horror films here with some of my favorite actors.
Alfredo: Really? I love horror films!
Bill: A fifty- year- old movie! Are you kindding?
Pat: Well, then, how about a western? Do you like westerns?

Bill: A western?
Alfredo: Wait a minute. I think I have I have an answer to our problem .
Pat: what problem?
Alfredo: Well , we can't agree on a movie, right?
Bill: Well,....
Alfredo: How about some music? Theres a terrific group at the Cate Solo tonight.
Bill: Yeah. That sounds good.
Pat: Sure. Why not?
Alfredo: Well' then , let's go!

Bill: So , what's the name of this rock group?
Alfredo: it,s not a rock group . it's a country and western group.
Bill: Country and western?
Alfredo: Yeah.
Bill: Well , gee , I... I really don't like country and western very much....
Pat: Isn't there a jazz concert at the City Center tonight?
Bill: Jazz? Do you really like jazz?

What's your favorite kind of music?

People talk a bout their preferences in music as they listen to and watch live performances.

Reporter :Hi . I'm Austene Van Williams ,and I'm in front of a country and western nightclub.
Lets talk to some people and see what they
Think of the music .

Reporter : How do you like this music ?
Woman 1 : We love it . we love it .
Reporter: What kind of music do they play here ?
Woman 1 : country. Country music .
Reporter : And how often do you get to go to
Nightclubs?
Woman 1 : Well , we just come here mostly about …uh, two times a week .
Reporter : What's your favorite kind of music ?
Man 1 : country western .
Reporter : country western ?
Man 1:Yeah .

Reporter : What's your favorite kind of music ?
Man 2 : country western . The old time , hard – core country western . western swing . And my least favorite is rap .
Reporter : Rap?
Man 2 :I…I don't understand it . It makes me feel old .

Reporter : What's your favorite kind of music ?
Woman 2: I really enjoy country music . I like a variety of music , though , so …
Reporter : How often do you listen to live music ?
Woman 2: Um … couple of times a month , maybe .

Reporter : What's your favorite kind of music?
Man 3 : Uh … if I say country – no , it's not country . It's probably jazz.
Reporter : jazz?
Man 3 : Right .
Woman 3 : Uh …jazz .

Reporter : What kind of music do they play here ?
Woman 4: They play jazz .
Man 4 : Uh… almost always jazz . Some blues.
Reporter : What's your favorite kind of music?
Man 5 : My favorite's older rock , uh, new wave . I like jazz a lot , too .
Woman 5 : I like classical music and jazz.
Woman 6 : I like jazz music , and I also like rock and roll.
Man 5: I like jazz music .
Reporter : How often do you go to nightclubs ?
Man 5 :Um , I come here about once a month .

Man 5 : I don't like country western music .
Woman 5 : I don't like country music , and I don't like rock and roll.
Man 4 : I really dislike Top 40 .
Reporter : Do you play a musical instrument yourself ?
Man 4 : No, I don't .
Woman 6 : Yes , I do . I play the guitar
Man 5 : I play saxophone .
Woman 5 : Yes , I play piano.

Reporter: I think the people here may have a few different opinions about music… How do you like this music?
Man 6: I enjoy it a lot.
Reporter: What kind of music do they play here?
Man 6: A lot of rock. A lot of R & B. It's usually good music.
Reporter: How often do you go to nightclubs?
Man 6: Pretty often do you go to nightclubs?
Reporter: How often do you go to nightclubs?
Man 7: Mm … once a week, maybe. .
Reporter: What's your favorite kind of music?
Man 7: Rock.
Reporter: Rock?
Man 7: Yes.
Reporter: What do you think of country and western music?
s OK, but'**Man 7**: Uh … it's not my favorite. It
I don't buy it, and I don't listen to it too'Idon
often, though.
Reporter: **Do you** play a musical instrument yourself?
Man 7: Um-hmm.
Reporter: What instrument is that'?
Man 7: The guitar.
Reporter: The guitar? Well, thank you very much
Man 7: **You're welcome.**

Reporter: What kind of music do they play here?
Woman 7: Great music. Dancing music

Reporter: And that's what people think of the music here. I think I'll go back for some more rock and roll. Bye now.

5 A family picnic

Rick invites Betsy to a family picnic .

Betsy : So , how many people are there in your Family , Rick ?
Rick : A lot , if you count all my cousins .
Betsy: Do they all live here in the States now ?
Rick : Oh , no . I have relatives in Mexico . My Grandmother and grandfather are there , and My older sister , too .
Betsy : How many sisters do you have ?
Rick : Two , plus an older brother . There's my Brother Freddy over there with his wife Linda.
Betsy : Oh , really . what do they do ?
Rick : Freddy has an impot –export business , and Linda manages a boutique .
Betsy : Is that their daughter ?
Rick : Yeah . Her name's Angela.
Betsy : She's cute . How old is she ?
Rick : She's three.

Rick : Betsy , I'd like you to meet my mother and Father.
Betsy : pleased to meet you .
Mrs . Hernandez : Hi , Betsy.

Mr. Hernandez: Nice to meet you , Betsy.
Betsy: Hello , Mr. Hernandez.
Rick : And this is my younger sister Cristina .
Cristina : Hi, Betsy .
Betsy : Hi , Cristina .
Rick : Aunt Marta , this is my friend Betsy Scott ,From the night school class.
Betsy : Hi .
Aunt Marta : Well , nice to meet you , Betsy . Can You two please come with me ? It's time for the Family picture .
Rick : Sure .
Aunt Marta : Come on , please , everyone

Betsy : Can I take the picture for you ? Then you Can be in it , too .
Aunt Marta : Oh , thank you Betsy ! Now here's The camera . I hope it works OK. It's … it's An old one .
Betsy : Oh , no problem …. Listen , everybody . I Want you to say " cheese" on three . One …Two …. Three!
Family : Cheese!

6 I like to stay in shape.

Mark tries to impress Anne by telling her about his fitness routine

Mark : Hi there . Nice day , isn't it ?
Anne : Oh , yes , very nice.
Mark : Do you often come out here this early ?
Anne : Usually . I like to stay in shape .
Mark : I do , too . I usually get up around five o'clock .
Anne : Oh, really?
Mark : Yeah , I usually start with some stretches . There's a great aerobics program on Tv at six .
Anne : No kidding . I guess you really do like to stay In shape .
Mark : Hey , three days a week I go straight to my Health club after work .
Anne : Wow . What do you do the other two Evenings ?
Mark : Tuesdays and Thursdays , I'm on the old tennis courts by five –thirty.
Anne : Well , after all that exercise during the week , What do you do over the weekend ?
Mark : Saturday and Sundays are my days for Team sports.

Mancy : Hi , Anne . Are we late ?
Anne : Oh ,no , Nancy . You're … right on time . Hi ,Terry.
Terry: Are you ready for a couple more miles ?
Anne : Sure . Say ,… would you like to join us ?
Mark : Oh , no ….Uh, thanks , anyway . I don't have Time today . Sorry .
Anne : OK. Well , bye – bye . Have a nice day !

Mark : (to new person) Hi there. Nice day , isn't it?

7 How was your trip to San Francisco?

Phyllis tells Yoko about her trip to San Francisco.

Yoko : Hi , phyllis .
Phyllis : Hi , Yoko . How have you been ?
Yoko : Oh , fine . How about you ?
Phyllis : Great ! just great!
Yoko : So how was your trip to San Francisco?
Phyllis : Fantastic ! We really enjoyed it .
Yoko : Well, that doesn't surprise me . I love to visit San Francisco .Uh , So , your husband went With you?
Phyllis: Yes . I worked on Friday , and Bill had Business to do in the city , too.
Yoko : Oh , that's nice . So what did you do over the Weekend?
Phyllis : We went sight – seeing together all day Saturday and Sunday morning .
Yoko : Oh , really ? Tell me about it .
Phyllis : Well , we did a lot of interesting things . Naturally , we Started Saturday morning with A ride on a cable car.
Yoko : Naturally ... And then?
Phyllis : Then we went Straight to Ghirardelli Square to do Some Shopping .
Yoko : Isn't it wonderful ? I went there the last time I was in San Francisco .
Phyllis : Oh , it Sure is . We were there for a couple Of hours .
Yoko : Did you buy anything ?

Phyllis : just Some postcards and chocolate . We Didn't want to have too much to carry.
Yoko : What did you do after that ?
Phyllis : We had lunch at a crab stand at Fisherman's Wharf.
Yoko : Did you visit Alcatraz Island ?
Phyllis : No , we didn't have time .
Yoko : Oh ,.... What did you do then ?
Phyllis : We took a cab to Golden Gate Park .
Yoko : Great! Did you see the japanese Tea Garden ?
Phyllis: Oh , yes , it was really beautiful .... But to Tell the truth , the thing we liked the best was Chinatown.
Yoko : Oh , really ?
Phyllis : Yes . We went there on Sunday morning .
Yoko : What did you like about Chinatown ?
Phyllis : What did you like about Chinatown?
Phyllis: Well . ... all the people ,... and the Buildings , the Shops , and restaurants ... even The way the streets look . It was just a Fascinating place . We walked for hours .
Yoko : I know what you mean . It sounds like you Really had fun .
Phyllis : Oh , we had a great time! So how about You? What did you do over the weekend ?
Yoko : Oh , nothing much . Well , here we are again.
Phyllis : Oh , back to the real world !

8 Are you sure it's all right?

Bill invites two friends to a party and finds out that he has made a mistake .

Sandy : Are you sure it's all right for us to go to the party ?
Bill : Of cours I am. Katy's a good friend of mine.
Sandy : Yes , but she didn't really invite pat and me , and it is a little late .
Bill : It's OK , Sandy . It's a very informal party ,...
And anyway she knows both of you already .
Pat : OK . Well, we're at the corner of 31st Street . Now what ?
Bill : well , I don't remember her address, but I know she lives near here .
Pat : Fine . But do I go left , right , or straight ahead ?
Bill : Straight ahead ....I remember there's a movie theater just before you turn .
Pat : Hey , is that it ?
Bill : No , I don't think so ....There was a coffee shop next door and a drugstore across the street.
Sandy : Oh, I don't see a drugstore . well , there's a Vietnamese restaurant .... With a book store next to it.
Pat : Yeah , and no coffee shop either . Hey , look ! There's another movie theater up ahead on the left .
Bill: Great ! There's a drugstore .

Bill: We're almost there .... Turn left at the corner ....
There's a parking lot just to the left ....There it is !
Pat : Great !

Pat : So where does Katy live ?
Bill: In one of those apartment buildings across the street .
Pat : which one ?
Bill: It's the one on the corner .

Sandy : And you're sure it's all right for us to arrive this late ?
Bill: come on , Sandy !
Sandy : I don't hear any music !
Katy : Bill?
Bill : Hi. Katy.
Katy: Hi.
Bill : Are we too late for the party ?
Katy : Oh , no ....Uh , actually , you're a little early.
Bill: Really ?
Katy: Yes . The party is next Friday .
Bill: Next Friday .
Katy: Yes . Hi , Sandy . pat . come on in .
Sandy : I'm sorry , Katy.
Pat : Are you sure it's all right ?
Katy: No problem ....It looks like we have a party here tonight after all .

In a suburban home

A woman talks about her home as she walks through each room .

Reporter : Homes in North America come in all shapes and sizes . Hi . I'm Donna Fox . Today we're going to look at a typical home in the midwestern United States . Homes are often very large in the Midwest .As you can see, there's a lot of room to build houses here . The Bartlett family lives in this two – story suburban home . Let's go inside and meet Marcy Bartlett.
Reporter : Hi, Marcy. Thanks for inviting us to see your house .
Marcy : Your's welcome , Donna . Thank you for coming.
Reporter: Are you ready to begin our tour ?
Marcy : Sure . This , of course , is our kitchen , where we have most of our family meals .
Reporter : How many people are in your family ?
Marcy: There's four: my husband Bob , my two children , and myself .
Reporter : What other rooms are on th ground floor?
Marcy : Well , we have the formal dining room right through here .
Reporter : And when do you use this room ?
Marcy : We use it mostly for entertaining and special family dimmers .
Reporter : It's lovely
Marcy : Thank you .
Marcy : And we have our living room here on the main floor also .
Reporter : Oh , I like it ! what's on the second floor ?
Marcy : We have four bedrooms upstairs . would you like to go and see?
Reporter : Yes.

Marcy : And this is my son Matthew's room . He's five .
Reporter : Oh, it's really nice !
Marcy : And over here we have the guest room .
Marcy: And down here we have the children's bathroom
Reporter: OK.
Marcy: And over here is my son Daniel's room .....
He's eight .
Reporter : Oh ....Oh , your son has lots of trophies . Where did he get them ?
Marcy : He tades karate .
Reporter : He takes karate .
Reporter: Oh .
Marcy : And through here ...is our bedroom .
Reporter : Well, you have lots of room up here .
Where does the family spend the most time ?
Marcy : Oh , that's easy , Donna. Down in the family room . Come on and I'll show you
Reporter : OK
Reporter :What a great family room !
Marcy : Thank you . The boys love to play down here , and we spend a lot of time watching TV, playing games ...
Reporter : Well , thank you so much for the tour , Marcy .
Marcy : You're welcome , Donna . Thank you for coming .

9 Help is coming.

Sarah and Dave are relaxing at home when they are surprised by visitors.

Sarah: Would you like another cup of coffee?
Dave: No thanks . I don't think so.
Sarah: Is there anything interesting in the paper?
Dave: Well , theres something about a prison escape.
Sarah: Oh, really?
Dave: Yeah. Acouple of guys escaped from the state prison in a gray van.
Sarah: Hmm....Do we know anyone with a minivan?
Dave: A minivan? What color is it?
Sarah: I don't know Light blue , maybe , or gray. I can't see very well.
Dave: where is this van?
Sarah: Its parked right in front of the house .
And there are two guys in it
Dave: Oh, really?
Sarah: Now theyre getting out of the van
Dave: What do they look like.
Sarah: Well,... one man's tall , and I think he has blond hair ,He's wearing a baseball cap.
Dave: How about the other one?
Sarah: He's ... short ... He's got dark hair. Now they're coming up the driveway.
Dave: Sarah, you keep watching. I'm going to call the police. _____
Sarah: I think that's a good idea.

Dave: What are they doing now?
Sarah: They've stopped in the driveway and they're just looking around.
Dave: about how old are they? Can , can you tell?
Sarah: well , the tall one looks like he's about twenty , and I guess the short one's in his late forties Oh, Dave, now they're coming up to the door. Hurry!
Dave: it's all right , Sarah, Help is coming.
Sarah: Wait a minute! I can really see them now... oh, Dave! ... The short one is your cousin George.
Dave: My cousin George!
========

George: Dave! So this is the right address. It's been so long since I've seen you, I wasn't sure.
Dave: George! What on earth are you doing here?
Sarah: please, come in?
George: we were passing through town and decided to stop and say hello , You haven't seen Don here since he was a baby.
Don: Hi.
Sarah: Well, It's great to see you both again...
Dave , I think you should make that phone call, don't you?
Dave: Uh, sure please excuse me a minute.
Sarah: Dave'll be right back come in and sit down.

10 Sorry I'm late.

On his way to meet Marie , Tom has a problem.

Waitress: Good evening.
Marie: Hi , There will be two of us... thank you.....
Tom: Marie! I'm really sorry. How long have you been waiting?
Marie: Its ok , Tom I've only been here for a little while . Is everything all right?
Tom: Yes , it is now , but you want believe what just happened to me.
Marie: well , what happened?
Tom: Well , first of all, I was a little late leaving my apartment , and so I was in a hurry . Then , Just after I started the car, I was in a hurry. Then , just after I started the car, I remembered I didn't have any money with me, so I went back to get my wallet.
Marie: Did you find it?
Tom: oh , yes I found it . That wasn't the problem the problem was when I got back to my car , I couldn't get in.
Marie: Do you mean you locked your keys in the car?
Tom: That's right . so ,guess what I did after that!
Marie: I can't guess.
Tom: First I tried to call you, but there was no answer.... Than I called one of those twenty. Four- hour lock services ..... And they sent a man over to help me.

Marie: And he opened your car door for you?
Tom: that's right.
Marie: How long did it take?
Tom: About two minutes. So, I paid him and came straight here...
Marie: How much did this cot you?
Tom: oh, it wasn't very expensive. It cost only- oh , no!
Marie: what is it?
Tom: My wallet! Its still in the car!
Marie: oh!
Waitress: Good evening. Are you ready to order now?
Marie: Don't worry, Tom You've had a hard day, And it's my turn to pay , anyway.
Tom: thanks.
Marie: Let's see....
Tom: well , should we start with an hors d'oeuvre?
Marie: Hm- hmm
Tom: ok

Across the Golden Gate Bridge

Mr. And Mrs. Chang get directions and advice as the rent a car at the airport.

Ken: Good morning. May I help you?

Mr. Chang: Yes. We're here to pick up a car.

Ken: Do you have a reservation?

Mr. Chang: Yes. The Nane is Chang.

Ken: Ok Chang; Here it is , Mr: Change Paid in advance. Sign here and here. And that's for one week then?

Mr. Chang: That's right. One week.

Ken: Are you staying in san Francisco?

Mrs. Chang: No, we're going to visit friends in the Napa Valley.

Ken: Oh, NAPA Valley. That's one of my favorite places. The wineries and vineyards there are some of the most famous in California.

Ms. Chang: What's the best way to get there from here?

Mrs. Chang: Yes, and are there any interesting places to visit along the way?

Ken: The most interesting way is across the Golden Gate Bridge. It's not too crowded this time of day, and you can stop in Sausalito for lunch.

Mrs. Chang: Sausalito?

Ken: Yes. It's a fascinating little town just across the bridge. You should definitely see it.

Mrs. Chang: Can you recommend a good restaurant?

Ken: I really like HoUlihans. It's right on the waterfront, and there's a wonderful view of San Francisco across the bay.

Ms. Chang: So Sausalito is on the way to the Napa Valley?

Ken: Yes , it is And so is Muir Woods. You should stop there for a while, too , if you have time.

Mrs. Chang: Muir Woods?

Ken: Yes It's a beautiful redwood forest. You shouldn't miss it.

Mrs. Chang: Mum. Sounds interesting.

Ms. Chang: Well, thank you for the information. Wed better go find our car now.

Ken: That will be easy. Take the shuttle bus, Just outside the door to the right. Here is your contract and directions to help you find the Golden Gate Bridge. Do you need anything else?

Mrs. Chang: No. we have everything that we need Thank you so much.

Ken: Ok. Good- bye. See you next week.... Oh, And be sure to visit one of the wineries up in Napa Valley.

Mr. Chang: Thanks . We will.

Mr. Charg: I just remembered. I don't have a map of the Napa Valley. Maybe I can get one here.

Mrs. Chang: Don't worry, dear. We can get one in Sausalito after lunch.

12 feeling bad

Steve receives various home remedies for his cold from his co-workers.

Sandy: How are those papers coming for this afternoon, Steve?
Steve: Nearly finished.
Sandy: Do you still have that cold?
Steve: Yeah, its still pretty bad , Sandy.
Sandy: Listen, I've got just the thing for you. Just a second…. Here.
Steve: What's that?
Sandy: Its something I picked up at the health. Food store. You just mix it with hot water and drink it.
Stevey : But what is it?
Sandy: I'm not really sure. I think it has ginseng in it or something like that. Try it.
Steve: Are you sure it works?
Sandy: of course it does.
Steve: Well, thanks, Sandy. That's really nice Maybe later.
Sandy: Ok… Oh, but don't drive after you take it.
Steve: Why not?
Sandy: It makes you sleepy.
Steve: sleepy?
Sandy: Yeah, its pretty strong medicine.

Jim: Hey, Steve. Still feeling bad?
Steve: Yes it's this terrible cold.
Jim: No problem. I have something for you.
Steve: You do? Great.

Jim: Yeah, it's here in my briefcase. My mom makes it for me when I have a cold.
Steve: Really?
Jim: Here it is. Try it.
Steve: Umm. Thanks Jim ….Uh, what is it?
Jim: it's garlic juice. Actually, Its garlic, onions, and carrots.
Steve: Great.
Jim: its garlic juice . Actually, its garlic, onions and carrots.
Steve: I'm sure. Gee, Thanks, Jim.
Jim: Not at all…. Hope you feel better.
Steve: Thanks.

Rebecca: Well, Steve. How are you feeling now?
Steve: Oh, about the same, Rebecca.
Rebecca: Oh …Listen, don't take any of this stuff. I have the best cure of all.
Steve: You do?
Rebecca: That's right . Im taking you out to lunch to a place where they make the best chicken soup in the world.
Steve: What a good idea.
Rebecca: it is. So come on, lets go
Steve: You know, that's the best advice I've had all day, Rebecca. Just give me a minute to clean my desk. I'll meet you downstairs, OK?
Rebecca: Ok . See you in a minute.

At the Mall of America

People talk a bout the largest mall in North America as they look and shop

Reporter: Hi there. This is Neil Murray speaking to you from the Mall of America in Bloomington , Minnesota. And what is the Mall of America , you ask? Would you believe the biggest shopping and entertainment mall in the entire United States? Here at the Mall of America , you'll find four major department stores, all under the same roof .... Plus, hundreds of other places to shop. There are fourteen cinemas....More than forty places to eat ....There's dancing. There's music... And in the middle of everything . There's Camp Snoopy, an exciting amusement park.

———

Report: Now , let's ask some people what they're doing here.... Is this your first time at the Mall?
Woman 1: Yes , it is.
Reporter: why are you here?
Woman 1: For Camp Snoopy , mainly. It's been really fun We did a little bit of shopping and...
Reporter: What do you think people should do first when they come to the Mall of America?
Woman1: Wear tennis shoes ! ... Wear tennis shoes . I didn't wear them.

———

Reporter: Have you been to the Mall of America before?
Woman 2: Uh yeah , about three times.
Reporter: Why are you here now?
Woman2: Because my mom came in from Ohio , and she wanted to go to the Mall of America.
Reporter: Have you purchased anything yet?
Woman2: Yes I bought a pair of shoes.

———

Reporter: What would you recommend for visitors from another country?
Woman3: Well , this is a great place to come. I mean, there's everything. It's got everything in it , so if there's anything specific you're looking for, you can find it here.

———

Reporter: Hi.
Young girls: Hi
Reporter: Whts your name?
Ashley: Ashley.
Reporter: And you?
Corina: Corina.

Reporter: Where are you from?
Ashley: Oklahoma.
Corina: Oklahoma.
Reporter: What did you do when you got here?
Corina: We rode rides and looked at the stores.
Reporter: Have you eaten any food yet?
Ashley: No, we were too busy on the rides.

———

Reporter: May I ask you your name?
Hernando: Hi. Hernando.
Monica: Monica.
Rodrigo: Rodrigo.
Reporter: Where are you from?
Rodrigo: I m from Ecuador. That's in South America.
Monica: Me, too Ecuador.
Hernando: I am from Colombia, in South America, too.
Reporter: Why are you here at the Mall of America?

Hernando: Ah, for shopping. Just now for shopping.
Reporter: Have you bought anything yet?
Rodrigo: Yeah. Just a couple of tapes.
Reporter: well, where are they?
Rodrigo: They are over here...Just the tapes. We're beginning.
Monica: Because we just arrived a few minutes ago.
Reporter: Are you having a good time?
All: Yeah

———

Reporter: Can you describe the Mall of America in one word?
Woman1 : Wonderful!
Woman4: Big . Real, real big!
Man: Outstanding!
Boy 1: Fun!
Boy2: Good!
Women: Great!

———

Reporter: And that's the way it is, here at the Mall of America. This is Neil Murray saying, Why don't you come and see for yourself?

13 At the state fair

Various people enjoy a day at the fair .

Steve :oh , corn on the cob , I love that . we always
Had that at the fair when we were little .
Liz : we did , too .
Vendor 1 : Hey , this is the place! Get your fresh
Corn on the cob here! Fresh , hot –roasted corn
On the cob !... what would you like ?
Steve : I'll have one of those , please .
Vendor 1 :coming up … what about you ? would
You like one , too ?
Liz : Not right now , thank you . I'm not hungry .
Steve : Maybe you should give us another one ,
Anyway !
Vendor 1: Sure .

===

Nancy : oh , he is so cute !
Rick : Yeah , but that was a lot of work . Now let's
Find a place to eat .
Betsy : How about over there ? There's a restaurant
Where we can sit down , too . My feet are
Tired … You can keep the dog with you .
Rick : oh , all right .(to stuffed dog)come to papa,
Yeah . Aw , good boy . Yuh !
Waitress : Hi ! May I take your order ?
Betsy : Yeah , I think I'll have a hot dog and a small
Order of french fries .
Waitress : would you like anything to drink ?
Betsy : I'll have a small diet cola .
Waitress : OK .And what can I get you ?
Nancy : I guess I'd like a salad plate and a cup of
Tea , please.

Waitress : what kind of dressing would you like on
That ?
Nancy : Do you have Thousand Island ?
Waitress : Yes , we do . would you like anything
Else?
Nancy : No . that'll be all , thanks .
Waitress : Thank you . And how about you ?
Rick : A hamburger, a large order of fries , and a
Chocolate milk shake ,please .
Waitress : Any thing else ?
Rick : How about something for our little friend ?

===

Paul : I'm glad that's over .
Cynthia : I'm hungry . How about you ?
Paul : I don't know . I don't think so .
Cynthia : oh, look ! They're selling ice-cream
cones !
Vendor2 : Hi . what'll you have ?
Cynthia : I'd like a cone , please .
Vendor2 : How many scoops?
Cynthia : Three , please .
Paul : Three scoops ?
Cynthia : Yes , one for me and two for you!
Vndor2 : Thank you.
Cynthia: see , I knew you wanted some.

Marlene , jack , and Kathy are contestants in a game show .

Announcer : And now it's time to play "Around the World"
With your host johnny Traveler.

Johnny : Ladies and gentlemen , welcome to
"Around the world." the game show about
world geography . And now , let's meet our
piayers.

Announcer : Acomputer engineer from Seattle ,
Washington , Marlene Miller ! A high school
Teacher from Boston , Massachusetts, jack
Richardson ! And from Vero Beach , Florida , an
Accountant , Kathy Hernandez!

Johnny : Welcome to "Around the world" . And
Now , let's begin our game . our categories are
Deserts and Mountains , Rivers and
Waterfalls , Oceans and Islands , Cities and
Countries . Marlen , please begin .

Marlene : I'll try Rivers and waterfalls for fifty ,
Johnny .

Johnny : Which is longer , the Nile River in Africa Or the
Amazon River in South America?...
Jack ?

Jack : Um ...Um ...the Nile .

Johnny : That's right for fifty !Next category ,
Please .

Jack : OK, I'll try Deserts and Mountains for fifty
Johnny.

Johnny : which is higher ,Mt McKinley in North
America or Mt . Kilimanjaro in Africa ?
Marlene .

Marlene : Mt . Mckinley .

Johnny : That's right . Your category , please ,
Marlene .

Marlene : I'll take Cities and Countries for fifty Johnny.

Johnny : what country is sometimes called the "island
continent" ?... Kathy .

kathy : Australia !

johnny : That's right for fifty . Your category .please .

kathy : I'll take Deserts and Mountains for one hundred ,
johnny .

johnny : what is the largest desert in Asia?...jack .

jack : oh , I know the answer . It starts with G....Go ...
Go... Gobi !

Johnny : Yes , the Gobi Desert ! wonderful! You
Have one hundred points . The next category Please ,
jack .

Jack : Cities and countries for a hundred .

Johnny : what is largest city in North
America ? ... Kathy .

Kathy : New York!

Johnny : No . Good try ... jack .

Jack : Uh ... Los Angeles ?

Johnny : No . Sorry , jack . Marlene .

Marlene : Mexico city .

Johnny : That's right for one hundred . Your
Category , Marlene ?

Marlene : I'll try Rivers and waterfalls for one
Hundred , johnny .

Johnny : Angel Falls is the highest waterfall in the
World . what country is it in ? ... jack .

Jack : Uh ... Brazil.

Johnny : No . I'm sorry , jack .... Kathy.

Kathy : Uh ... colombia !

Johnny : No , that's not correct , Kathy ... ,Marlene.

Marlene : It's Venezuela , johnny .

Johnny : That's right! You have one hundred
Points . Next category . please , Marlene .

Marlene : Oceans and Islands for fifty , johnny.

Johnny : Ooh !That's the end of our game . Let's
Look at the score . Hey , it looks like Marlene
Has won . Congratulations , Marlene.

Marlene : Thanks , johnny .

Johnny : Now , Let's see what you've won.

Announcer: Marlene , you've won tickets for two
On Countryside Airlines , the friendliest airline
In the sky ,to one of the most exciting ,
Beautiful , fascinating cities in the country ...
Seattle , Washington!

Marlene : But I live in Seattle , Washington !

Johnny : Ooh ...well , that's our show ! Until next ti
Time , I'm johnny Traveler for Around the
World"!

15 May I speak to Cathy?

Cathy's father is trying to work , but the phone keeps ringing .

Mr . waite : (phone rings .) Hello?
Kevin : Hello , may I speak to cathy ?
Mr . waite : I'm sorry . She's not in just now .
Kevin : Is she coming back soon ?
Mr . waite : Uh , yes , I think so .
Kevin :well , could you tell her that kevin called
And that I'll call back later ?
Mr . waite : Sure, kevin .
Kevin : Thank you . Good – bye .
Mr . waite : Bye ...(writes message .)kevin will
Call back.

——————

Mr . Waite : (phone rings .) Hello ?
Jenny : Hello , Mr. Waite .This is jenny . Is cathy
Home?
Mr . Waite : oh , hi , jenny . No , cathy's not here
Right now .
Jenny : will she be back soon ?
Mr . waite : Uh, I'm not sure . would you like to
Leave a message ?
Jenny : well , could you just tell her to call me when
She comes in ?
Mr . Waite : Sure , I'll tell her . Bye , jenny .
Jenny : Bye , Mr . watite .
Mr . waite :(wright message.)call Jenny

——————

Mr . waite : (phone rings.) Hello?
Rachel : Hi , this is Rachel . Is cathy home ?
Mr . waite : Uh , no , she's not , Rachel . would you
Like her to call you when she comes in ?
Rachel : Yes , please . she has my number .
Mr . waite : I'll tell her , Rachel .Bye .
Rachel : Bye .
Mr . waite : OK .(writes message.) OK . Call Rachel.

——————

Cathy : Hi , Dad . I'm home !
Mr . waite : Hi , cathy .

——————

Cathy : Have there been any calls for me?
Mr . Waite : just a few ! kevin called . He'll call back.
Jenny called . She wants you to call her . And
Then Rachel called . She wants you to call
Her . too.
Cathy : Great!
Mr . Waite : The messages are next to the phone .
Cathy : oh , OK ... (phone rings .) I'll get that ...
Hello? ... Uh , no , actually he's busy righy
Now ... oh ,OK . I'll call him , then ...Dad,
It's your boss . He said it's urgent .
Mr . waite : All right . I'm coming .
Cathy : just a moment . He's coming .

——————

Cathy : Dad , are you all right ?
Mr . waite : I'm OK . I'm OK.
Cathy : just a moment .

——————

Mr . waite : john speaking ... oh no , no! Uh
No problem ! No problem at all!

16 A whole new Marty

Marty change his image and makes new friends.

John : I'm just terrible at calculus . I don't
Understand anything in this chapter .
Marty : I know what you mean . It is a tough coure .
John : Did you figure out the answer to this problem ?
Marcy : That's in chapter 11 . I did that last week .
Let's see.
Michelle : Hi, john . I see you're working on
Calculus .
John :oh , hi , Michelle . Yes , I am . Michelle , you
Know Marty , don't you ?
Michelle : Yeah , hi , marty . say , john , I 've got a
Couple of questions about chapter 12 .Do you
Want to study together ?
John : well , uh , actually , I'm still on chapter 11,
But Marty here is working on chapter 12.
Michelle : oh , that's OK. Actually , I've got to go to
Class right now . See you later .
John : OK , Michelle . See you .
Marty : Gee , john , how do you do it ?
John : what ?
Marty : Girls . They always talk to you . They never
Even notice me .
John : That's not true .
Marty : Yes , it is . Listen , I need some advice .
John : Well , maybe you could cut your hair .And
Your clothes … I don't know . They could be a
Little neater .
Marty : I see what you mean .
John : You need to be more outgoing . Maybe you
Should exercise . Then you'd have more
Energy .
Marty : Well , when do we start ?
John : well , how about right now ?
Marty : OK .Sound good to me .

Michelle : Hi , john . How are you ?
John : oh , hi Michelle .
Michelle : Do you want to study together for the
Calculus exam ?
John : Well , actually , I have to study for my history
Exam right now . But maybe Marty has some
Time .
Marty : Hi , Michelle .
Michelle : Marty ?
Marty : Yeah .
Michelle : I didn't recognize you !There's something
Different about you . Did you change your
Hairstyle ?
Marty : well , it's a little shorter .
Michelle : Hmm , maybe that's it . well , anyway,
Would you like to study for the calculus exam?
Marty : Sure .No problem . when do you want to
Start?
Michelle : How about right now ?
Marty : OK.
John : Looks like Marty has a new friend .

What is American food?

People try to figure out what American food really is.

Reporter : Hello. Are you feeling a little hungry ? I am.
And there certainly are a lot of different
Kinds of food to choose from here ...
Japanese ,... Mexican ,... Italian ,... and
Maybe even ... American , whatever that is .
My name is jennifer Santoro , and I'm here to
Find out what people in the USA like to eat .
I'll be asking a lot of questions , and I may
Even get some good answers to a very difficult
Question : What is American food ?
California – style restaurants , like this one , are
Found all over the United States . These
Restaurants are known for their interesting
Use of fresh fruits and vegetables . You can see
The influence of many international cuisines,
For example , Mexican ,... japanese ,... and
Italian . Let's find out what people say about
Eating here .

═══════

Reporter : what did you have for lunch today ?
Man 1 : I had a chicken salad .
Reporter : And what's your favorite kind of
Restaurant to eat in ?
Man 1: Uh , I like these California restaurants .
Reporter : what did you have for lunch today ?
Man2 : Uh , I had a Caesar salad .
Reporter: So, what are you eating for lunch ?
Woman 1 : Uh , pasta .
Reporter : How often do you eat out in
Restaurants?
Woman 1 : Quite often , in Taiwan .
Reporter : How often , once a week , twice a week ?
Woman 1 : Almost every day .

═══════

Reporter : Almost every town and city has at least
One Chinese restaurant . This one is in a
Neighborhood shopping center , and it's well
Known for its lunch buffet .

═══════

Reporter : What are you eating today ?
Woman 2: I'm having Chinese food .
Reporter : What's your favorite kind of food ?
Woman 2 : I really do enjoy Chinese .
Reporter : How often do you go out to eat ?
Woman 2 : I go out several times a week , usually
Four or five times for lunch.
Reporter : what are you eating?
Man 3 : I'm having , uh , hot – and sour soup and
Kung – pao chicken .
Reporter : what's your favorite kind of food ?
Man3: Well , I enjoy Chinese food. I enjoy most foods, I
guess.
Reporter: What are you habing
Man3 : oh , probably five , six time a week ,
Minimum.
Reporter : what are you having ?
Woman 3 : I'm having the pork Szechwan . which is
One of the specials of this restaurant .

Reporter : what's your favorite kind of restaurant ?
Woman 3 : I like this restaurant .

═══════

Reporter : Sometimes in America you can mix a
Little music and food together , such as in this
German – style restaurant .

═══════

Reporter : So what did you have for lunch today ?
Woman 4 : I had , um , a salad , and I also had
Goulash , Bavarian goulash , which was
Very good .
Woman 5 : I had the , uh , German ... uh ...
Cabbage , and the , uh ... German potato
Salad ,... and it was excellent .
Man 4 : I had aGerman bratwurst .

Reporter : In all of the restaurants we visited , we asked
people what they thought was a
Typical American food .
Man2 : I think it's very much hamburgers and
French fries .
Woman 6 : pizza .
Woman 1 : Hamburger , hot dog .
Man5 : Steak .
Man 6 : A typical American food would be ... ah ...
French fries , hamburger , hot dogs...
Woman 2 : Hamburger and french fries .

═══════

Reporter : This restaurant specializes in typical
American hamburgers and french fries ...
And the fast service many Americans like ....
What are you having?
Woman 7 : Um , I'm having a hamburger , and French
fries , and a coke .
Man 7 : I think I'm going to order the hamburger ,
... cheeseburger , maybe.
Woman 8 : I'm having a cheeseburger , fries , and a
Coke .
Man8 : Uh , hamburger.

═══════

Reporter : So, what is American food ? One answer
Is... hamburgers! But as we've seen .
American food is really a lot of good things to
Eat from all over the world ... I'm jennifer
Santoro , and now . I'm going to eat!